KINGDOM KINDNESS

KINGDOM KINDNESS

A MOVEMENT TO BRING CALM TO THE CULTURE

TONY EVANS

BETHANYHOUSE

a division of Baker Publishing Group
Minneapolis, Minnesota

Published by Bethany House Publishers
Minneapolis, Minnesota
BethanyHouse.com

Bethany House Publishers is a division of
Baker Publishing Group, Grand Rapids, Michigan

Printed in the United States of America

Library of Congress Cataloging-in-Publication Data
Names: Evans, Tony, author.
Title: Kingdom kindness : a movement to bring calm to the culture / Tony Evans.
Description: Minneapolis, Minnesota : Bethany House Publishers, a division of Baker
    Publishing Group, [2024]
Identifiers: LCCN 2023048237 | ISBN 9780764241994 (cloth) | ISBN 9781493445172 (ebook)
Subjects: LCSH: Kindness—Religious aspects—Christianity. | Courtesy—Biblical teaching.
Classification: LCC BV4647.K5 E93 2024 | DDC 177/.7—dc23/eng/20240129
LC record available at https://lccn.loc.gov/2023048237

Cover design by Faceout Studio, Jeff Miller

Baker Publishing Group publications use paper produced from sustainable forestry practices and postconsumer waste whenever possible.

24 25 26 27 28 29 30   7 6 5 4 3 2 1

This special book is joyfully dedicated to my new wife, Carla Evans, who exudes God's spirit of kindness everywhere she goes and to everyone she meets.

CONTENTS

INTRODUCTION

A Crisis of Meanness

Our culture and our world today are dealing with a virus of meanness. Whether on social media, in the workplace, on news channels and podcasts, or in the arguments that take place between people, meanness dominates the atmosphere. It even shows up in shoppers who are dissatisfied and in angry drivers. A mindset of entitlement has led people to believe that their "truth" is more important than other people's treatment or well-being.

Over and over again, we are witnessing this absence of civility becoming normalized in our environment, families, and relationships. It started to develop and grow around election seasons over the past decade, when name-calling and finger-pointing became part and parcel of general discourse. It then grew during the pandemic and lockdown, when all limits on judging others who might disagree with you—and guidelines on how this was done—were lost. Respect and kindness quickly gave way to accusation and insult. Over the years, the way we treat people and talk to and about them has become toxic, releasing the effects of bitterness, shame, resentment, and pride into the culture more than ever.

During this time, God put it on my heart to emphasize a spirit of kindness to others. It started at the church where I pastor. We developed and printed Acts of Kindness cards so members of the congregation could have a tool to share kindness in the culture. This card was meant to accompany an act of kindness for a stranger or a friend, which then offered the opportunity for prayer and the presentation of the gospel. Over the years, people's lives were impacted, and many people came to the church as a result of receiving these acts of kindness.

That's when the Lord put it on my heart to initiate this same Kindness in the Culture strategy through our national ministry, the Urban Alternative. Since launching the campaign, we have given out hundreds of thousands of cards as we seek to create a ripple effect of change in our culture. The goal is to transform the environment and the atmosphere from one of meanness to one of kindness and love.

This book is meant to help in this process by showing what kindness is, why it matters, and how God calls us to love others for the glory of His name. When we understand and apply principles of kindness, we will discover that God's blessings can even boomerang back to us. Kindness is good for everyone! Especially for the person who offers it. It is my hope and prayer that we, as kingdom followers of Jesus Christ, can live as leaders in inspiring a cultural shift so that kindness and love can become normalized in the way we live our lives and relate to one another in God's name.

I hope you will become part of this movement by doing acts of kindness, praying for people, and making sure they hear the gospel and thus also increasing your reward in heaven and blessings on earth. All of this comes together through simple, yet intentional, acts of kindness.

Tony Evans, Dallas, Texas

ONE

CREATED FOR KINDNESS

The fourteenth-century Black Death plague has gone down in history as the most fatal pandemic ever. In just a few years, this deadly infection claimed the lives of tens of millions of people worldwide. Many state that it killed half of Europe. Some cities lost as much as 80 percent of their population.survival rates among those who came into contact with the bacterium *Yersinia pestis* ranged around 30 percent on average.[1]

The plague spread quickly, bringing with it excruciatingly painful symptoms with little hope for relief. Whether touched by the pain of illness or the pain of grief and loss, no one in Western Eurasia or North Africa escaped its wrath.

The COVID-19 pandemic that began in 2020 also sent global shockwaves, changing everything in its course. And while not comparable to the bubonic plague or many other plagues of earlier centuries, due to advances in medical science, it still wreaked havoc on our world. I know few people who were not impacted by this pandemic through either the loss of a loved one (or multiple loved ones) or a loss of the normalcy of life and work routines. Yet COVID-19 is not the only deadly virus we are contending with today. There exists a pandemic of similar force and destruction. It is the pandemic of meanness that has taken our world by storm.

This pandemic has arisen out of political division, racial division, online bullying, and general societal upheaval. It fuels an atmosphere of vitriol, hatred, and dishonor. Disrespect in speech and action has become normalized in our culture. We are consumed by selfishness, leading to a smash-and-grab mentality, whether in word or deed. The internet has devolved into a cesspool of negativity, giving space for Satan's strategies of division to not only take root but flourish. Cancel culture exemplifies this me-first mentality, which seeks to remove anything and everything that disagrees with the "approved" status quo.

It would be one thing if I were talking only about the unsaved taking part in this pandemic of meanness. But it's not only the unsaved. Christian social media sites often do not differ from the rest. Judgment, accusation, and insult are integral parts of this pandemic. In fact, I know some unsaved individuals who are nicer than many Christians. I know several who are less self-centered, proud, and divisive. Unfortunately, many in the body of Christ have joined the contemporary culture in failing to reflect the Spirit of Christ in relating to others. They have fallen prey to a pandemic spread through germs of hate and conceit.

All pandemics have an origination point. This pandemic of evil is tied to a grave sin that Scripture calls selfishness. Selfishness and grandiose self-focus have elevated vices that damage relational behavior above the kingdom virtues of kindness, love, and gentleness. Now, I understand that no one is perfect and we all sin. There will be days when your game, or my game, is not fully on. But when ill behavior becomes the norm for a large number of people—or the collective body of Christ comes to be known for ill behavior—we have a pandemic.

Our culture is disintegrating at warp speed with this prevalence of meanness. We live in harsh times driven by self-centeredness when everyone's "truth" competes with that of others. Our news media are filled with this same kind of evil that, for many reasons, has penetrated the atmosphere with a stench of division. Yet as believers made in the image of God, we were not created for meanness. We were created for compassion. We were created for kindness. The Bible says in Romans 2:4, "Or do you think lightly of the riches of His kindness and tolerance and patience, not knowing that the kindness of God leads you to repentance?" In other words, God has not carried out His wrath on any of us as we deserve. He doesn't react every time we sin or blow it. He doesn't blast us every time we fail. Due to God's kindness, He is patient and tolerant while He waits for us to come to a place of repentance. He doesn't cancel us when we mess up. God's kindness models how we have been created to live. Kindness is to be the hallmark of who we are.

> GOD DOESN'T CANCEL US WHEN WE MESS UP. GOD'S KINDNESS MODELS HOW WE HAVE BEEN CREATED TO LIVE. KINDNESS IS TO BE THE HALLMARK OF WHO WE ARE.

Psalm 117:2 says, "For His lovingkindness is great toward us, and the truth of the LORD is everlasting. Praise the LORD!" Great is the kindness of God. It is in kindness that we are not destroyed, given the holiness of God and our failure to live up to His standards. God is kind even to "ungrateful and evil men" (Luke 6:35).

We read more about God's kindness in Psalm 119:76, which says, "O may Your lovingkindness comfort me, according to Your word to Your servant." Kindness offers comfort and reveals to us the caring heart of our Father in heaven (see Exodus 34:6). Because of God's kindness, we live and move and have our being (see Acts 17:28). Thus, as His followers and kingdom disciples, kindness is to be our modus operandi. It is to be how we operate—how we roll.

As children of the King, we are to live as ambassadors of God's kindness. God doesn't want His followers to be merely nice. He wants us to be kind. Nice can be a persona or a personality. But kindness requires action. Kindness is what you do to and for others in your niceness. Kindness is niceness on display. In fact, people ought to know how nice you are by how kindly you talk, walk, and behave. When kindness is a mindset, it shows up in what you do. Routine and regular acts of kindness can penetrate the culture, creating a new and fresh atmosphere of love, acceptance, and peace. Kindness is the visible demonstration of love as we seek to benefit others in God's name.

A number of years ago, the church where I pastor had a problem in our Education Center. Shortly after it was built and opened, we noticed a continual stench in one of the restrooms. It reeked with a putrid smell that, despite all our attempts at cleaning, just wouldn't go away. We called on internal teams to address it. When they couldn't remove it, we brought in external crews to address it. We paid for professional cleaners to change the atmosphere that had not just settled in the bathroom but had also leaked out into the halls of the school. A funk soon began to fill the entire building.

The smell remained, not due to a lack of trying to remove it. It remained because nothing we did to remove it worked. We funded the project to remove it. We engaged professionals to remove it. But the stench stayed. It wasn't until one of our custodial staff noticed something very simple, which everyone else had ignored. He noticed that the fan in the ceiling was turning the wrong way. So instead of pushing the stench out into the vented areas, the fan forced the smell into the restroom. When the custodian turned the fan so that it went in the right direction, the heart of the problem was solved.

There is a stench in our culture today. The atmosphere is thick with incivility and strife. Despite all the funding aimed at making a better society and all the attempts to quell the issues by validating everyone, the problem remains. This is because we have too many people with hearts turning in the wrong direction. When hearts turn away from God and His kingdom values, chaos results. No amount of money, effort, or programs will solve the chaos caused by a removal of God's values from culture. It is only when our hearts are in alignment with God that we will see the effects of an atmosphere teeming with life.

Philippians 2:1–7 shows us the ingredients of a heart like Christ's. We read,

> Therefore if there is any encouragement in Christ, if there is any consolation of love, if there is any fellowship of the Spirit, if any affection and compassion, make my joy complete by being of the same mind, maintaining the same love, united in spirit, intent on one purpose. Do nothing from selfishness or empty conceit, but with humility of mind regard one another as more important than yourselves; do not merely look out for your own personal interests, but also for the interests of others. Have this attitude in yourselves which was also in Christ Jesus, who, although He existed in the form of God, did not regard equality with God a thing to be grasped, but emptied Himself, taking the form of a bond-servant, and being made in the likeness of men.

Had Jesus been selfish, no one would be saved. No one would be on their way to heaven. Rather, it was because of Jesus' heart of love, kindness, and surrender that He did not hold tightly to His rightful position. He "existed in the form of God" but "did not regard equality with God a thing to be grasped." Instead, He gave himself up as a sacrifice for humanity's sins. In this passage Paul urges us to "have this attitude" in ourselves that Jesus modeled for us with His life and death.

God is not opposed to self-interest. Self-interest is not sinful. *Selfishness* is sinful. We see this in the passage we just read. Paul writes that we are not to "merely look out for" our own personal interests. That tells us that it is okay to make sure we are okay. You can make sure things are working out for you. There's nothing wrong or sinful about that. But what is wrong and sinful is to look out for *only* yourself. To be concerned with only how you are doing is selfish. If you are a person who wants to be blessed but never desires or offers yourself to be a blessing to someone else, that is wrong. Selfish saints do not contribute to a better society. This is because selfishness is rooted in a lack of love for others. Love builds up a culture because the attributes of love contribute to healthy lives and relationships.

First Corinthians 13 tells us what love comprises. One of the most important aspects of love is kindness. We read in 1 Corinthians 13:4, "Love is patient, love is kind and is not jealous; love does not brag and is not arrogant." In other words, if you are unkind, you do not love. Love *is* kind. If you are mean to someone, you do not have love. If you are unkind to your spouse or hateful in your speech to your spouse, you do not have love. You can say "I love you," but it means nothing if it is not tied to actions of love—actions rooted in kindness. The love that comes from God is kind. Love doesn't put someone down. Love doesn't reduce someone's dignity through words, mean actions, ignoring the person, or excluding them. Love is niceness in function, not in philosophy.

Watch What You Say

If you live in Texas as I do, you will become acquainted with some significantly hot weather in the summer. Texas summers can be similar to winters in other regions in the way people make it a point to always stay indoors or in a car to get someplace else that will also be indoors. No matter where you live, however, thermostats are important, and they are important all year round because they regulate the indoor temperature. When it's cold, we want to be able to raise the temperature. When it's hot, we want to be able to lower the temperature. A thermostat governs the atmosphere. Wherever you are, the thermostat is adjusted to affect the environment.

As a Christian, you have a role in affecting the environment. You are to serve as a spiritual thermostat, helping to regulate the atmosphere toward one of love. While you alone can't control the temperature of the unrighteous or the culture at large, you are able to control the thermostat of your own heart. If and when enough Christians join together to regulate the thermostat of love, through kindness, we will influence society as a whole. A thermostat of saints can spread God's love. God expects us to demonstrate His love to others through our good words and our good works.

Paul talks about these good words in Ephesians 4:29–32, which says,

> Let no unwholesome word proceed from your mouth, but only such a word as is good for edification according to the need of the moment, so that it will give grace to those who hear. Do not grieve the Holy Spirit of God, by whom you were sealed for the day of redemption. Let all bitterness and wrath and anger and clamor and slander be put away from you, along with all malice. Be kind to one another, tender-hearted, forgiving each other, just as God in Christ also has forgiven you.

The bottom line of that passage is this: Watch your mouth. Be mindful of what comes out of it because the words you say can actually grieve the Holy Spirit of God. There should be no committed kingdom follower of Jesus Christ who is known for his or her profanity, vitriol, insults, or hate speech. Colossians 4:6 says that all of our words should be "as though seasoned with salt." They should be tasty, digestible, and palatable. That includes what you say on social media.

When I was a water safety instructor decades ago, I had to do mouth-to-mouth resuscitation on a drowning victim. I had to help them breathe again by giving breath into their body with the life that was in mine. We need Christians today who know how to use their mouths to enable others to live and thrive again. We need to speak grace to the hearer, and truth influenced by love. All truth should be couched in a spirit of love so that it doesn't come across as vitriol. Love lets the other person know that you care and that what you are saying is spoken with a heart to help, not hurt. Rather than just venting about the state of our nation or society, we need to minister to others through what we choose to say.

> WE NEED CHRISTIANS TODAY WHO KNOW HOW TO USE THEIR MOUTHS TO ENABLE OTHERS TO LIVE AND THRIVE AGAIN. WE NEED TO SPEAK GRACE TO THE HEARER, AND TRUTH INFLUENCED BY LOVE.

Just turn on the television or stream content for any length of time and you will quickly become horrified at what passes for normal language. People are being downright evil to each other in what they say and post online these days. You and I are not to be caught up in that. We're not to adopt that way of living, because that's not who we are in Christ. We are to reflect Jesus Christ in all we say and do. Your words should make it clear that God controls your tongue.

Not Just What You Say, but What You Do

In addition to good words, we are to be known for good works. Matthew 5:16 says, "Let your light shine before men in such a way that they may see your good works, and glorify your Father who is in heaven." Good words should always be followed up with good works.

In fact, 1 Timothy 6:17–19 explains that if God has blessed you, you ought to use that blessing to bless others:

Instruct those who are rich in this present world not to be conceited or to fix their hope on the uncertainty of riches, but on God, who richly supplies us with all things to enjoy. Instruct them to do good, to be rich in good works, to be generous and ready to share, storing up for themselves the treasure of a good foundation for the future, so that they may take hold of that which is life indeed.

You have been created by God for good works that will glorify Him and bring benefit to those around you (see Ephesians 2:8–10). What you do and what you say ought to demonstrate the kindness of God to a world steeped in meanness. At the height of the pandemic, everyone was worried about how contagious the virus was. What we need right now is a positive contagion of kindness to permeate our culture and spread like a ripple on a pond. It ought to spread through everyone who names Jesus Christ as their Savior. We are to intentionally seek opportunities to reflect the love of God in all we do.

Keep in mind, good works are different from good things. Sinners can do good things. Atheists can do good things. Pagans can do good things. You don't need to be a Christian to do a good thing. Non-Christians build hospitals and orphanages and do acts of philanthropy. But as believers in Christ, we are called to do good works, not just good things. While a good thing is done to help somebody, a good work is performed to help somebody to the glory of God and in His name. When God is not attached to the good you do, then it is only a good thing. But you and I have been called to carry out "good works." The temporal, physical good work leads to the eternal, spiritual opportunity for God to manifest himself to the person or people impacted. Our good works are to bring God the glory He deserves.

A biblically defined good work seeks to do three things:

1. Bring people into the kingdom through salvation in Christ (evangelism, 1 Peter 3:15).
2. Help people become more useful for advancing God's kingdom agenda on earth (discipleship, Matthew 28:19–20).
3. Benefit the people of the kingdom in their various situations in life, helping them to improve a scenario or circumstance in God's name (service, Proverbs 25:21).

When you do something nice, that is good. But when you do a good work, you are inviting a spiritual, eternally lasting reality into the social, emotional, or physical need. You are pursuing the addition of a spiritual benefit to the good thing. Here's an example to help clarify this further: Imagine you are standing at an elevator and you see the door open only to discover there is no elevator car to step into. If you were to step forward, you would end up in a disaster down below. So you step back and find yourself safe and saved because you made a choice based on what you saw.

Now, if you are still standing near the elevator, and around the corner walks a blind man toward the same elevator, there is a need in front of you. What's more, you notice that his right shoe is untied. But he can't see that. Out of concern that he will trip, you ask if you can tie his shoelace. That's a very good thing to do. When he replies that you can, you bend down and tie it. You are relieved, because you don't want to see him trip and fall.

But then, when he feels for and presses the elevator button, and the door opens to reveal that yet again there is no car, you choose not to say anything about it. You don't mention to the blind man that there is a big drop ahead should he walk through that elevator door. And while it's true you did a good thing by tying his shoe so that he would not trip, you've only helped him for a moment. You have not helped him toward his destiny, because you've now allowed him to walk through the door to the carless elevator shaft.

There are many good things we can do to help people. But when we fail to attach helping a person for eternity (their spiritual destiny) to such a deed, it is only a good thing for a moment. We can tie shoelaces all day, but if it is only so that someone can walk more quickly and safely to their doom, that doesn't make a whole lot of spiritual sense. God has called us, rather, to do good works in the areas of evangelism, discipleship, and service. In this way, we glorify Him and improve the spiritual well-being of those whom we have helped.

If you are poor and you don't have enough income to make it, that's bad. At some level, you can receive help in order to recover from poverty. And if you are homeless, that's bad. But also at some level, you can receive help to keep you out of the rain or heat or cold on bad-weather days. But if you die without a saving faith in Jesus Christ, you've just been hit with a blow from which you cannot recover. That's why a good work can't just be about niceness. It must be attached, as much as possible, to the spiritual realm or it is only a temporal patch on an eternal crisis.

Loving Others as God Loves Them

Hebrews 13:16 puts it like this: "And do not neglect doing good and sharing, for with such sacrifices God is pleased." By being a blessing, you will open yourself up to be blessed. By serving others, you draw closer to the heart of God himself. God desires to use you to advance His kingdom agenda on earth. The primary foundation of His kingdom agenda is this: LOVE. We are to love God and love others. Love is made manifest through kindness. As we read earlier in 1 Corinthians 13:4, "love is kind." God wants kindness to be our watchword as believers. It is to be a defining quality. He wants kindness to be the atmosphere we create wherever we go. Whether it is in what we post or how we comment on social media or what we say in conversation—or how we treat others in lines or while driving—whatever the case, kindness should dominate our thoughts and actions.

We live in a culture where anyone and everyone can become an instant celebrity on social media. But there are to be no celebrities in Christianity other than God himself. We should all think, and act, like servants. This is the way we are to live that Jesus modeled for us. Even if you are treated like a celebrity, you should think like a servant. You should function like a servant. You should seek to do all the good you can by all the means you can in all the ways you can in every place you can at all the times you can for all the people you can in the very best manner you can. This heart, mindset, and lifestyle of kindness will bring God the glory He deserves.

TWO

CULTIVATING COMPASSION FOR OTHERS

Much of what we study as we look at the subject of kindness in the culture revolves around an important question. It's a question that often appears in our own hearts and minds as we navigate this gift called life. Maybe we word it differently from one another, but the essence can be summarized as follows:

What matters most? *or*

What do I need to prioritize? *or*

What does God want from me? *or*

What is my purpose?

All these questions show up within us from time to time. It's only natural. We want to find out where we need to invest our time and energy, and why it even matters to do so. No one likes wasting his or her days or getting to the end of their life only to discover that it all meant nothing. The question of why we are here and what we are to do with the lives given to us is one we all seek to answer at some point or another.

Even those who did not follow Jesus as His disciples while He walked on earth wrestled with these questions. Their questions came out on occasion, often disguised as a test. But if I were to guess, there was some level of sincerity in their queries. One of these is recorded for us in the book of Matthew, posited by a lawyer.

For the lawyer to approach Jesus and ask this question was nothing out of the ordinary. He had spent his life studying and applying what he had learned of the law. He had invested his days in what he thought would make a difference. He may also have chosen this career so he could advance socially and have a comfortable place to live, a secure home for his family's legacy. But at the end of the day, he knew there had to be more.

The context of the question involves Pharisees gathering to try to trick Jesus and trip Him up. But one wonders whether the lawyer who asked the question really did want to know the answer himself. Because he phrased it like this: "Teacher, which is the great commandment in the Law?" (Matthew 22:36).

Jesus' answer didn't trip Him up at all, though. His answer gave no room for the Pharisees to accuse Him. What's more, it shed light on what matters most—to the Pharisees and to all of us. The Pharisees had sought to test Him with the question, but instead they opened the door for Him to give all of us the way to living a pure, holy, and meaningful life. We read His reply:

> And He said to him, "'YOU SHALL LOVE THE LORD YOUR GOD WITH ALL YOUR HEART, AND WITH ALL YOUR SOUL, AND WITH ALL YOUR MIND.' This is the great and foremost commandment. The second is like it, 'YOU SHALL LOVE YOUR NEIGHBOR AS YOURSELF.' On these two commandments depend the whole Law and the Prophets."
>
> Matthew 22:37–40

The first part of Jesus' reply lets us know our highest priority in life: To love God passionately and righteously. We are to make pleasing God the most important thing we can do. But Jesus added the second commandment, even though the Pharisees had not asked for it: We are to love our neighbor as ourself. To love one's neighbor is to compassionately and righteously seek the well-being of another without expecting anything from them in return.

YOU Are the Neighbor

In another of the gospels, we read a similar account in which a lawyer approaches Jesus to test Him. After Jesus had spoken in private to His disciples, the lawyer stood up to publicly ask his question. It is in Jesus' answer that we all discover to whom we are to show kindness and what it means to be a neighbor. We read in Luke 10:23–29,

> Turning to the disciples, He said privately, "Blessed are the eyes which see the things you see, for I say to you, that many prophets and kings wished to see the things which you see, and did not see them, and to hear the things which you hear, and did not hear them."
>
> And a lawyer stood up and put Him to the test, saying, "Teacher, what shall I do to inherit eternal life?" And He said to him, "What is written in the Law? How does it read to you?" And he answered, "YOU SHALL LOVE THE LORD YOUR GOD WITH ALL YOUR HEART, AND WITH ALL YOUR SOUL, AND WITH ALL YOUR STRENGTH, AND WITH ALL YOUR MIND; AND YOUR NEIGHBOR AS YOURSELF." And He said to him, "You have answered correctly; DO THIS AND YOU WILL LIVE." But wishing to justify himself, he said to Jesus, "And who is my neighbor?"

The lawyer sought to justify himself by narrowing Jesus' answer down to what he considered a reasonable response. He had begun by asking how he could inherit eternal life, a question rooted in self-preservation and self-actualization. Yet the conversation wound up focused on personal justification. The lawyer had shifted from testing Jesus to seeking to justify his own life, wanting to receive the benefits, blessings, and rewards of the eternal realm. It had become personal.

Jesus' reply was equally personal and shed light not only on what the lawyer must do to expand and grow in knowledge and spiritual understanding, but on what we need to do as well. The lawyer had asked who his neighbor was. Yet Jesus' reply answered his question in an entirely different way. Through His example, we discover what it means to *be* a neighbor to someone else. We read Jesus' response in verses 30–37:

> Jesus replied and said, "A man was going down from Jerusalem to Jericho, and fell among robbers, and they stripped him and beat him, and went away leaving him half dead. And by chance a priest was going down on that road, and when he saw him, he passed by on the other side. Likewise a Levite also, when he came to the place and saw him, passed by on the other side. But a Samaritan, who was on a journey, came upon him; and when he saw him, he felt compassion, and came to him and bandaged up his wounds, pouring oil and wine on them; and he put him on his own beast, and brought him to an inn and took care of him. On the next day he took out two denarii and gave them to the innkeeper and said, 'Take care of him; and whatever more you spend, when I return I will repay you.' Which of these three do you think proved to be a neighbor to the man who fell into the robbers' hands?" And he said, "The one who showed mercy toward him." Then Jesus said to him, "Go and do the same."

Jesus didn't directly tell the lawyer who his neighbor was. Rather, Jesus revealed that the lawyer himself was to be a neighbor to anyone in need. The definition of *neighbor* in this explanation is "the one who showed mercy toward him." What's more, the *him* who received the mercy was not someone the neighbor would normally have associated with, so that left the door open to being a neighbor to everyone in need.

For cultural context, the Samaritans and the Jews were known enemies. Jesus intentionally chose an example of someone in need whom the lawyer, as a Jew, would not naturally seek to help. We learn from this passage that living as a neighbor involves seeking to help those whose needs you see and whose needs you are able to meet, regardless of social circle, background, race, or any other such criteria.

The context of this story gives us insight into how we are to show kindness to others. The man in the story was walking from Jerusalem to Jericho, which is about a seventeen-mile walk. Not only is it a long walk, but it is also a steep decline. There is a more than three-thousand-foot decline over the walk from Jerusalem to Jericho. This trek involved a winding and treacherous road that offered plenty of places for robbers to hide.

> **LIVING AS A NEIGHBOR INVOLVES SEEKING TO HELP THOSE WHOSE NEEDS YOU SEE AND ARE ABLE TO MEET, REGARDLESS OF SOCIAL CIRCLE, BACKGROUND, RACE, OR ANY OTHER SUCH CRITERIA.**

As this man journeyed, he fell into the hands of thieves, who messed him up pretty badly. They beat him, robbed him, stripped him of all he had. The man was left half-dead. He could no longer help himself because he was weak and bleeding and may even have been unconscious.

While this man's story involves a physical robbery, it also illustrates a spiritual reality that so many people live today. Myriads of people are living a half-dead kind of life. They are half-dead because they have been robbed of their freedom, dignity, or even innocence. They may have been abused, misused, manipulated, and taken advantage of. Whatever the case, they've been lied to and have wound up at a loss. Whether they've been stolen from by the circumstances of life, predatory lenders, gold diggers, or get-rich-quick schemes, they now find themselves stripped of all they once had, and they are destitute.

Even worse off are those who have robbed themselves through their own poor choices based on impulse, hormones, or emotions rather than on godly wisdom. These poor choices stole life via sin and rebellion against God's revealed and preferred will. Whenever decisions are made outside of God's will, you not only steal from yourself and your future, but also steal from your legacy. These losses can pile up over time and can keep people from functioning properly as adults. Sure, they are still alive, but they are also half-dead. In other words, they are no longer experiencing all that life was meant to give.

When someone finds themselves in this situation and they see no way out of the mistakes they've made or the deception they've been duped by, they need help. They need outside intervention. They need someone who is kind enough to step in and help them get back on their feet. That's what the man who had been beaten by the robbers needed. Both a priest and a Levite walked by, and the man may have felt some hope when he saw them. He needed them. He needed their help and their compassion. But neither of them gave him so much as the time of day. Even though both saw this man's need and both had the capacity to meet the need, because they did not feel compassion for him, they walked on by.

Even though these men's jobs were to serve the law of God, and they had just come from Jerusalem, which would indicate they had just left the temple or synagogue, they ignored God's teaching on helping others. When they happened upon a half-dead man beaten up and tossed to the side of the road, neither said or did anything at all—other than cross over to the other side of the road to avoid him.

We aren't given the reasons the priest and the Levite walked by, but we can take a guess. Perhaps they thought the robbers and thieves were still in the vicinity. They might not have felt it was safe to stop. Maybe they even thought it was a trap.

Another reason could have been that they were trying to keep the law that prohibited them from touching a dead body. Even though the man wasn't dead yet, they could have assumed he was going to die and didn't want to become unclean in the process of assisting him. Yet another possible reason for their not stopping is simply the inconvenience of it. They could have had a schedule to keep, a plan to achieve, or a meeting to get to. All of these might seem like legitimate reasons to pass by the beaten and bruised man, at least from their perspective. And so they did.

But the Samaritan felt compassion for the man. As a result, he stopped to help. He bandaged his wounds. He poured oil and wine on his body. He placed the man on his own animal to transport him to an inn for further treatment and care. The following day, he even paid the innkeeper to continue to look after the man until he was well. Even though the injured man was a Jew and an enemy of the Samaritan people, the Samaritan knew and demonstrated what it meant to help someone in need.

The priest and the Levite were Jews themselves. There was no division between them and the man who had been robbed. Culturally, it was far more natural for them to help the man. Spiritually, it was also more natural for them to help the man. And yet they didn't. They were too busy. Or too scared. Or too apathetic. Rather, it was the Samaritan who saw the man in need and acted upon his compassion for him.

The lawyer had hoped to trip Jesus up with his clever question. But Jesus simply flipped a different question back to him. The man had asked, "Who is my neighbor?" But Jesus responded with, "Who proved to be a neighbor?" The man had tried to justify himself out of having to help people. He wanted to identify a presumably smaller segment of people he needed to help, so he could subsequently ignore the needs of the rest of the population. But Jesus flipped the script, emphasizing which person proved to be a neighbor. In doing so, Jesus let us know that each of us is called to be a neighbor. We are called to live in such a way that when we see a need and have the means to meet it, our neighborly response is to feel compassion and help. The priest and the Levite saw the need. They had the capacity to meet the need. But they did not act as neighbors by feeling compassion and providing help. To love is to compassionately and righteously pursue the well-being of another. We are called to love everyone. John 13:35 says, "By this all men will know that you are My disciples, if you have love for one another."

Jesus made it clear that the neighbor was the one "who showed mercy" and that we are to "go and do the same." Being a neighbor is not complete until mercy has been extended. To show mercy is to act compassionately to relieve misery. This is how we are to live. It is to be how we roll. Once you realize that kindness and love are not optional but a way of life for those who follow Jesus Christ, it will change your outlook. It will open your eyes and give you insight into God's work in your own life. God desires to bless those who bless others in need.

Blessing Others Blesses You

What many people do not realize is how this great commandment of love, and living as a neighbor, produces life-giving results in their own lives. We often think that being kind to others is a one-way street. Maybe we consider kindness an act of charity—something to cross off our list. But Scripture tells us that what we do to and for others has a profound impact on the quality of our own lives. When you realize that your actions toward others directly affect your own life, you will take them more seriously.

God is looking for individuals who are not so focused on promoting or serving themselves that they are unwilling to reach out and touch the lives of others. He is looking for people who will bring hope to the culture, in addition to help. He's seeking people He does not have to beg, prod, and nudge to serve but who will serve out of the love in their hearts. People who will not discriminate regarding who they help, when they help, or why they help.

Jesus explained to us through the parable of the good Samaritan that a neighbor (the person we are to be) is one who shows love and mercy to others. And we, as neighbors, are to help any person whose need we see and are able to meet, because if we love God but don't love people, we don't actually love God (see 1 John 4:20). The two are connected. People are made in the image of God. Thus, if you are mean to people, you are mean to God. If you are apathetic to people, you are apathetic to God. If you lack empathy or compassion for people in need, you lack empathy and compassion for God and His creation.

Jesus told the questioning lawyer that the two greatest commandments are to love God and to love others (see Luke 10:27). When the lawyer sought to clarify who, exactly, was his neighbor and who he was to love, Jesus showed that he was asking the wrong question. After all, compassion does not discriminate. Compassion is your willingness to help the person who needs help and whose need you are able to meet.

Many people today have been robbed by wicked people and practices, personal choices, catastrophes, inflation, abandonment, and all manner of evil—just as the man in the parable had been attacked and robbed. And while the priest and the Levite (who had just come from the synagogue) did not feel anything for the man in need, the Samaritan did. The priest and the Levite had been too holy to be kind. Too busy to be kind. Too uppity. But the good Samaritan saw a man, one from another racial group, whose need he could meet. He felt compassion and took the time to show kindness.

It's true that you cannot meet every need in the world, but when God reveals a need to you as you go about your day, and He has given you the opportunity to meet that need, you must do what you can to show kindness.

THREE

THE DIVINE IMPERATIVE

Most of us have been to the circus or have seen circus acts online. Or perhaps you've seen a show by Cirque du Soleil in which individuals perform daring feats. One of the acts regularly seen in these types of shows is the high-wire act. This involves a person walking on a wire from one location to another. Their hands grasp a pole to help steady themselves and keep themselves balanced. The wire is so thin that if they were to lean too far to one side or the other, they would fall off and meet disaster. So they try to avoid any tipping at all. To become too far out of balance on a high wire is to fall.

Unfortunately, today we are living in a world that is out of balance. People are tilting to one side or another, and then back again. They are tilting to cultural sides, racial sides, class sides, political sides, gender sides, and many others. There is so much out of balance in our nation today that we are witnessing a disaster of epic proportions. People are unable to walk out their lives in a straight line because they are being pulled to one side or another. Their equilibrium has become challenged. The church's equilibrium has become challenged as well, and Christians now struggle with this issue of balance.

On one side there are Christians who are so heavenly minded that they are no earthly good. They speak only of the glories of the life to come, while doing little to address the disasters in the life that is. On the other hand, there are those Christians who are so earthly minded that they are no heavenly good. They've become so secularized, culturalized, and worldly that heaven has no use for them. They fail to bring an eternal perspective or a kingdom agenda into what they do. Yet when the balance is off, few truly benefit at all.

God encapsulates this concept of balance and our need for it in one straightforward verse. It's a very well-known verse in Scripture, but just because it is well-known doesn't mean it is well-applied. This verse ought to frame our outlook on how we go about our lives. It's Micah 6:8, and it says,

> He has told you, O man, what is good;
> And what does the LORD require of you
> But to do justice, to love kindness,
> And to walk humbly with your God?

To put this verse in context, Micah is a book composed of a covenantal lawsuit. In it, God makes His formal, legal complaint against His people. His people were playing church while trying to bribe God with religion. That's why He leads up to this verse with rhetorical questions. We read,

> With what shall I come to the LORD
> And bow myself before the God on high?
> Shall I come to Him with burnt offerings,
> With yearling calves?
> Does the LORD take delight in thousands of rams,
> In ten thousand rivers of oil?
> Shall I present my firstborn for my rebellious acts,
> The fruit of my body for the sin of my soul?
>
> vv. 6–7

These questions punctuate and highlight what not to do when serving God. They sound right and they may even look right, but God's heart desires something more authentic. Have you ever gone to a restaurant only to have the waiter bring you something entirely different from what you ordered? If that has happened to you, the waiter probably apologized and went to fix the order. They didn't just set the food down in front of you and say, "Well, at least you get to eat!" That type of service is unacceptable. Similarly, the service that God's people were giving Him as recorded in the book of Micah was unacceptable. They were giving God religion, church attendance, and even their tithes. They were worshiping Him in a spirit of religiosity. But their performance was not what mattered to God. Because that was not what He had demanded of them. As King, God ought to receive what He wants. That's why Micah 6:8 is worded as an imperative. An imperative is not a request. It is a command.

God isn't *suggesting* that we do justice, love kindness, and walk humbly with Him. He isn't saying it's a nice idea. Nor is He asking that we do these things whenever we feel like it. Rather, God is *requiring* this. This is what serving God looks like. To live in another way is to live in disobedience to God, your Creator and King. When God laid out His demands to His people, He let them know that if they wanted Him to accept their religion, tithes, and worship, they would need to do justice, love kindness, and walk humbly with Him.

> GOD ISN'T *SUGGESTING* THAT WE DO JUSTICE, LOVE KINDNESS, AND WALK HUMBLY WITH HIM. HE ISN'T SAYING IT'S A NICE IDEA. NOR IS HE ASKING THAT WE DO THESE THINGS WHENEVER WE FEEL LIKE IT. RATHER, GOD IS *REQUIRING* THIS.

If you and I can embrace these three principles in our own lives, families, churches, and communities, we will witness God showing up for us. But if we refuse to assimilate them into our everyday experience, we will merely be carrying on with religion as usual. We will miss out on seeing God in a way that brings Him the greatest honor and glory.

The first of the three principles for kingdom living is to "do justice." It's important to notice that justice is something you *do*. It's not merely something you discuss. It involves more than having a workshop or seminar. Justice needs to be done or it is not justice. Questions about what justice is and how we carry it out often arise, and problems result when we don't share a common view of what it means to do justice. What I believe to be fair for me or for someone else may not be what you believe to be fair, and vice versa. These disagreements about what is fair have led to a significant amount of division in our culture and calamity in our society. Whether based on history, experiences, or perspective, people's views on fairness and justice differ. So while we are to "do justice" as kingdom followers of Jesus Christ, we first need to define what doing justice means to God.

In Scripture, the word *justice* often refers to doing what is right, doing things the prescribed way. Thus, biblical justice is "the equitable and impartial application of the rule of God's moral law in society."[1] Justice always starts with what God declares a matter to be. James 4:12 punctuates this when it says, "There is only one Lawgiver and Judge, the One who is able to save and to destroy; but who are you who judge your neighbor?" What is right and what is wrong is therefore determined by God.

Any rule made must be consistent with the one Lawgiver, God, and His rules, or it is an unjust rule. Chaos ensues when fairness and justice are defined outside of God's prescribed order. Here's one way to understand this: Imagine that you made certain rules for your home, but then those who live in your home decided to make their own. They made rules that excluded you from experiencing things in your own home, but that benefited them and their use of your home. Consequently, things would not be operating in your home the way you want them to. You would question how or why those who are living in your home would do this. It's your home, and you pay for everything they enjoy there. Similarly, God has made the world and all it contains. In order for things to flow smoothly in His world, we need to abide by His rules and His definition of justice.

When people seek to redefine justice in ways that benefit them while excluding God, they are looking out for their own interests. Oftentimes this also means excluding the interests of others too. That's why justice has to be impartial. It can't be tied to any one person's or one group's interest. Justice must be anchored to something bigger than us as individuals. It must be tied to God and His standards for humanity. The moment governments or ruling entities begin to make laws that benefit one group of people over another, they have gone outside of God's prescription for justice. They are decreeing that which is inconsistent with the King, His kingdom, and how He has designed history to work.

God has given us all we need to live according to His will and His ways. He has established His rule from the heavens. He has combined justice with righteousness, love, and truth because you can't define justice apart from knowing what is right. The following verses describe it like this:

- "Righteousness and justice are the foundation of Your throne; lovingkindness and truth go before You" (Psalm 89:14).
- "The Rock! His work is perfect, for all His ways are just; a God of faithfulness and without injustice, righteous and upright is He" (Deuteronomy 32:4).
- "Lovingkindness and truth have met together; righteousness and peace have kissed each other" (Psalm 85:10).

Justice cannot exist apart from a right standard by which to measure decisions and actions. The two must always go together. And since God is a God of righteousness, all justice must flow from His rule and standards. Injustice is the refusal to equitably and impartially apply God's moral law in society.

Justice versus Pluralism

We're living in a period of pluralism. Pluralism winds up agreeing with the relativist view that the only absolute is that there are no absolutes. Pluralism declares that there are no superintending rules. We all get to make our own rules and are not defined by nor governed by a set of common beliefs. Any idea is as valid as any other idea. Basically, everyone gets to do what is right in their own eyes (see Judges 21:25). When every group gets to make their own rules and the rules of the various groups clash, you get chaos. With no governing guidelines to which all must submit, the result is a lack of peace, harmony, and productivity. We see this all over our culture today.

When God chastised His people for leaving His way, He started them back on the right track by demanding they do justice. Justice is the cornerstone of freedom. You cannot have freedom as it was meant to be without the establishment of and adherence to just boundaries. We desire fairness in economics, work environments, relationships, and more. And yet God says we cannot expect fairness if we choose to function apart from His divinely inspired, just ways. Only God's standards will promote a culture of fairness and equality. Within His standards we find freedom.

The church is to be the thermostat for the culture. We are to be the influencers. We're supposed to bring God's point of view to bear as we demonstrate God's character and love. Yet the church itself needs to fall in line under God's rule. We have kicked justice to the curb by allowing so many injustices to go unchecked, both in history and in the current day. The American church has often acquiesced to the culture in order to be accepted—for example, failing to address the injustices of slavery and Jim Crow in any meaningful way until the civil rights movement. More recently, the abortion issue has led to division in society and in the church, resulting in a lack of Christian impact on the culture as some placate the pluralism of choice when instead the church should be applying God's moral law in a whole-life justice agenda from womb to tomb.

Today we have the opportunity to do justice and righteousness for the sake of healing as well—for the culture and for the church of Jesus Christ. Pacifying a pluralistic society by having a black church, a white church, a Hispanic church, etc., is man's answer, not God's. We should not, in the name of love, abandon the truth, but we must choose to take a biblical stand, comprehensively and consistently bringing God's truth in love on each issue.

> WE MUST STAND UP FOR AND ENACT THE EQUITABLE AND IMPARTIAL APPLICATION OF GOD'S MORAL LAW, BASED ON HIS WORD, IN SOCIETY. WHEN WE DO THAT, WE "DO JUSTICE."

We must stand up for and enact the equitable and impartial application of God's moral law, based on His Word, in society. When we do that, we "do justice."

What It Means to Love Kindness

Second, the Micah 6:8 passage tells us we are to "love kindness." Justice is combined with kindness because if you are concerned only about justice, you can develop a hard heart. You can develop a coldness if your sole focus is law and order. Leaning too far toward justice without coupling it with kindness can cause you to fall from the tightrope of living a balanced life under God's rule. You've got to balance the pole in your walk of faith. Balancing justice with kindness produces stability, hope, and productivity.

The Bible often uses the root word *hesed* for kindness, or the compassion of God. We read this translated as "lovingkindness" in

Psalm 100:5, which says, "For the LORD is good; His lovingkindness is everlasting and His faithfulness to all generations." God doesn't solely lean toward justice. He balances it with mercy and love. This creates a culture of compassion. We should never seek to choose between justice and kindness. The two must go hand in hand.

God's kindness leads with love. Often it is shown toward those to whom life has not been so good. In Zechariah 7:4–10, we gain a glimpse into God's heart of love and kindness related to justice:

> Then the word of the LORD of hosts came to me, saying, "Say to all the people of the land and to the priests, 'When you fasted and mourned in the fifth and seventh months these seventy years, was it actually for Me that you fasted? When you eat and drink, do you not eat for yourselves and do you not drink for yourselves? Are not these the words which the LORD proclaimed by the former prophets, when Jerusalem was inhabited and prosperous along with its cities around it, and the Negev and the foothills were inhabited?'"
>
> Then the word of the LORD came to Zechariah saying, "Thus has the LORD of hosts said, 'Dispense true justice and practice kindness and compassion each to his brother; and do not oppress the widow or the orphan, the stranger or the poor; and do not devise evil in your hearts against one another.'"

Again, God combines justice and kindness in this passage. We are called to reach out to those in need and, to whatever degree possible, help them. There are so many people in our world today who are in dire straits, whether due to being abandoned by their parents, health problems, or other issues. God has asked each of us to step up and meet their needs out of a spirit of kindness and love.

One of the key principles in Scripture is that of showing mercy. Just as we all want to receive mercy from God, we are called to show mercy to others. Luke 6:36 says, "Be merciful just as your Father is merciful." In other words, when you cry out for mercy, God looks at your record of mercy toward others. He sees what you've done in this area. If you've shown no mercy to others, then He might choose not to show it to you. We have a responsibility to live obedient lives before God, and we are to pursue mercy in all we do. We cannot seek it for ourselves while denying it to others. That, in itself, is not mercy.

Mercy and justice have to be balanced. Not only must they be balanced in our external practices, but they must be balanced internally, in our relationship with God. We cannot expect to receive mercy from God if we refuse to share the same with those made in His image. We read about this in Matthew 18:23–35, which says,

> For this reason the kingdom of heaven may be compared to a king who wished to settle accounts with his slaves. When he had begun to settle them, one who owed him ten thousand talents was brought to him. But since he did not have the means to repay, his lord commanded him to be sold, along with his wife and children and all that he had, and repayment to be made. So the slave fell to the ground and prostrated himself before him, saying, "Have patience with me and I will repay you everything." And the lord of that slave felt compassion and released him and forgave him the debt. But that slave went out and found one of his fellow slaves who owed him a hundred denarii; and he seized him and *began* to choke him, saying, "Pay back what you owe." So his fellow slave fell to the ground and began to plead with him, saying, "Have patience with me and I will repay you." But he was unwilling and went and threw him in prison until he should pay back what was owed. So when his fellow slaves saw what had happened, they were deeply grieved and came and reported to their lord all that had happened. Then summoning him, his lord said to him, "You wicked slave, I forgave you all that debt because you pleaded with me. Should you not also have had mercy on your fellow slave, in the same way that I had mercy on you?" And his lord, moved with anger, handed him over to the torturers until he should repay all that was owed him. My heavenly Father will also do the same to you, if each of you does not forgive his brother from your heart.

This story is an excellent illustration of why it's important to be intentional about showing mercy to others. Every good thing given to us from God flows from His mercy. We do not deserve any of it. When God examines our hearts, He looks to see whether we seek to keep our blessings for ourselves or show love, mercy, and kindness to others. God has created each of us to live as a conduit of His blessing, not as a cul-de-sac. A conduit allows the blessing and favor of God to flow through us to someone else.

We must understand that while the content of the gospel is about the finished work of the death and resurrection of Jesus Christ, the scope of the gospel is that the poor would hear the good news. Jesus came that oppressed people would be set free. The power of the gospel is for eternity, but it is also so that people's lives will be improved on earth. When people embrace the glorious content of the gospel, they come to experience God's work in their lives through His people. Lives become better. People become free. As the body of Christ carries out the work of Christ through acts of justice and kindness and love, things improve. The eternal good news of Jesus Christ has been designed to change history. It is in showing the love of God to others that Christ's power is made manifest on earth.

The Power of Humility

Lastly, in addition to doing justice and loving kindness, we are to walk humbly with God. To walk with someone implies intimacy and relationship. God doesn't desire religion apart from the relationship tied to it. If there is no fellowship and intimate relationship, religion becomes an event, just something to cross off your list. To walk humbly with God indicates a willingness to follow Him and go where He is going. You can't walk with someone and go someplace other than where they are going. Walking together indicates an agreement in direction. As Amos 3:3 says, "Do two men walk together unless they have made an appointment?"

Adam and Eve walked with God in the cool of the garden. They were headed in His direction. Enoch walked with God as well. To walk with someone is to spend time with them and agree upon where you are going. If you've ever walked with a partner, you have probably talked along the way. The talking and the fellowship make the walking easier and the experience more pleasant. You are sharing life in motion.

When God asks us to walk humbly with Him, He is asking us to share our lives with Him in motion. To walk humbly indicates we are not the one choosing the pace or the direction. To walk humbly means we are going alongside the other, who is leading. God wants us to do life with Him. To talk with Him. To listen to Him. To learn from Him. The reason our prayers sometimes become boring is because we are not taking the time to listen to the response. We're just reciting a list of wishes. Imagine how that would seem if you did that with a human walking partner. I don't think you'd have a walking partner after doing that too many times.

God wants to hear from you, but He wants to hear from you in the context of a relationship. When you are walking humbly with God, you are telling Him about the good, the bad, and the ugly. You are talking with Him about the struggles, stresses, circumstances, and more. You are unveiling your heart to Him. Walking with God is a matter of faith and a matter of familiarity. One of the reasons we fail to hear God in our prayers is because we are too fixated on our own lists. We are not walking with Him as we would with a friend.

Walking is a term used to indicate communion with someone. Take walking a dog, for example. When your dog knows your voice and walks humbly with you, you don't need a leash. The dog will remain with you wherever you go. God desires that we remain with Him and walk humbly with Him—not bound by a leash of religious duty, but walking freely with Him out of love for Him.

To be humble doesn't mean to denigrate yourself. To walk humbly means you are willing to submit to divine authority. It means that no matter what anyone else says, you know the truth that God's sovereign hand is over all. You recognize that anything you have achieved in your life is a result of God's grace and mercy. You understand that God is over you. The only reason you are who and what you are is because of the goodness of God. When you realize that and hold to that truth, you walk humbly with the Lord.

God has given us a divine imperative. We are to do justice, love kindness, and walk humbly with Him. When we make this divine imperative our normal mode of operation, we will experience the fullness of His hand in our life. We will become a vessel through which His favor can flow. Kindness in the culture starts with a healthy balance of justice, love, and humility. When you learn to incorporate all three into the depths of your being so that they begin to show up in all you do, you will no longer have to try to be kind. You will no longer need to look for ways to impact culture for good. These things will come naturally to you because they will overflow from the wellspring of life and love in your spirit.

FOUR

SEEING BEYOND YOURSELF

Have you ever witnessed the entire atmosphere of a room change when someone walked in? If it was a person with a light and airy persona, maybe the atmosphere improved. But someone with a negative or sour demeaner can cause the atmosphere to become tense. Atmosphere matters, and it is impacted by more than we realize. The atmosphere in the home may be a better example. Have you heard the phrase "If mom is happy, the whole house is happy"? The atmosphere in which we live is sensitive to what is in it.

That's why the vitriol we witness being spewed across the news media, social media, and even our culture at large is damaging. It's not something to take lightly. If we, as followers of Jesus Christ, do not stand up for what is right, we will be contributing to the damage being done. We have a calling to impact and influence our culture for good and for the glory of God. One way we do this is by spreading an atmosphere of love through words and acts of kindness.

If you have a bad atmosphere in your culture, it doesn't matter how much money you spend on programs to fix society. If you have a bad atmosphere in your church, it doesn't matter how much you invest in community outreach. If you have a bad atmosphere in your home, it doesn't matter how big your house is or how fancy. That's because if you are making plans in an atmosphere with a stench, it doesn't matter how detailed or elaborate they are—no one will want to be around a stench. Atmosphere affects both effectiveness and enjoyment.

When God created the church, He was creating an environment to foster spiritual and familial relationships. He didn't create the church simply to be a classroom where you would receive instruction. Nor did He create it to be a theater where you come to watch a performance. God established the church to function as a community in which authentic Christianity can be lived out. In other words, He wanted the church to be a place where real people in real relationships are meeting real needs in real ways. We must reject and counter the unkindness that used to be part of our unredeemed lives and replace it with works of kindness (see Titus 3:1–3).

Don't Be Fake

Have you ever been to a carnival and seen cardboard figures with a hole in place of the face so people can put their faces for photo-ops? When I go to the Texas State Fair every year with my family, I see these alongside the rides and activities. Someone who wants to look muscular and fit can simply stick his or her head through the circle and get a picture with a whole new physique. But it doesn't take a genius to observe that the body doesn't fit the face. It may give off the impression of a full-body makeover, but it's clearly fake. We run into a similar problem spiritually when the body of Christ is paired up with the head, Jesus. The head and the body don't always, or even often, look like they belong together. That's why so many people no longer attend church—because they feel it is fake.

We are called to live authentic Christian lives, and one way we do this is in how we show love. Paul explains this in Romans 12:9–13:

Let love be without hypocrisy. Abhor what is evil; cling to what is good. Be devoted to one another in brotherly love; give preference to one another in honor; not lagging behind in diligence, fervent in spirit, serving the Lord; rejoicing in hope, persevering in tribulation, devoted to prayer, contributing to the needs of the saints, practicing hospitality.

As a reminder, *love* can be defined as "compassionately and righteously seeking the well-being of another." What Paul is urging us to do in this passage is to live out a life of love without a mask on. When he writes that our love is to be without hypocrisy, he is telling us to take off the mask of fakeness. The Greek word translated "hypocrite" here referred to an actor who wore a mask. In Greek theater, the same actor often played a number of different characters. There would be a pile of masks, and he would grab the one for the character appearing in the play at that moment. To do this was seen as normal and thus the term *hypocrite* simply defined this role of playing someone you were not.

Some of the best actors and actresses in our world today are in the church on Sunday. They arrive with a mask on. They fake concern or care for others, even piety. They also fake it when others ask how they are. "Fine, blessed by the Best" is a common phrase even though their world may be falling apart, and they are anything but fine at that moment. The reason so many people feel they need to wear a mask in church is because they are afraid of what will happen if they ever do unmask themselves. They are afraid of being criticized, critiqued, or judged. Yet the church was meant to be a place where authentic relationships could be lived out in community.

Far too many Christians resemble the moon. We enjoy our lit side and want to shine. We desire to be loved, appreciated, and valued. But we also have a dark side. The dark side reeks of selfishness, secrets, and scandal. To avoid showing anyone our dark side, we wear a mask. But wearing a mask is a problem because the Bible tells us that "God is Light, and in Him there is no darkness at all" (1 John 1:5). So if you choose to live your life behind the mask, you are not living in the light of God's presence. Removing the mask doesn't mean you have to be perfect. It means you have to be honest and authentic. We read further, in 1 John 1:6–10,

> If we say that we have fellowship with Him and yet walk in the darkness, we lie and do not practice the truth; but if we walk in the Light as He Himself is in the Light, we have fellowship with one another, and the blood of Jesus His Son cleanses us from all sin. If we say that we have no sin, we are deceiving ourselves and the truth is not in us. If we confess our sins, He is faithful and righteous to forgive us our sins and to cleanse us from all unrighteousness. If we say that we have not sinned, we make Him a liar and His word is not in us.

Coming to church just to get your praise on is not being authentic. We all have shameful areas of our lives or our thoughts that we need to confess to God and get real about. God is not fooled by fake prayers camouflaged with high-sounding theological platitudes. He already knows the details of your heart. He knows the truth about you. Trying to fake it with God doesn't work. In fact, when you choose to live like that, you hurt yourself. You limit your prayer life because when you only allow yourself to talk about the mask life in your prayers, there isn't a whole lot to say. Neither is there a whole lot of help to access. God wants you and me to tell Him the truth, to come clean with Him. The first step to loving others without hypocrisy is loving God without hypocrisy. You must first remove the mask with God before you can remove it with people.

> THE FIRST STEP TO LOVING OTHERS WITHOUT HYPOCRISY IS LOVING GOD WITHOUT HYPOCRISY. YOU MUST FIRST REMOVE THE MASK WITH GOD BEFORE YOU CAN REMOVE IT WITH PEOPLE.

After Paul reminds us to love without hypocrisy in Romans 12:9, the verse then gives us two parameters of love that we read earlier: "Abhor what is evil; cling to what is good." These boundaries show us how to demonstrate real love. Authentic love doesn't ignore evil. Nor does it ignore good. Authentic love (and kindness) calls wrong wrong. But it also calls right right. Love never negates the truth. This should be true in your own life. Skipping over your own wrongs and pretending you are something you are not doesn't belong in church. The community of Christ ought to offer an environment in which each of us can be loved without wearing a mask, where we don't have to put on a performance for *Showtime at the Apollo*. The Christian family ought to be one in which we accept each other, and ourselves, for who we truly are. When that is done, we are able to show love and kindness in the culture without hypocrisy.

Reflecting God to Others

In the book of 1 John, we see how critical it is that we reflect the love of God to others. It's not only critical for impacting the atmosphere with the love of God, but it is also critical as it relates to our own relationship with God. Much of what God decides to do with you, to you, or for you is predicated on what you do with others, to others, and for others. God does not want you to camouflage Him in your everyday life. He wants you to authentically reflect Him to those around you. The only way you can reflect God fully is in love and kindness, based on the biblical definitions of those words. We read more about this in 1 John 4:11–21, which says,

> Beloved, if God so loved us, we also ought to love one another. No one has seen God at any time; if we love one another, God abides in us, and His love is perfected in us. By this we know that we abide in Him and He in us, because He has given us of His Spirit. We have seen and testify that the Father has sent the Son to be the Savior of the world.

Whoever confesses that Jesus is the Son of God, God abides in him, and he in God. We have come to know and have believed the love which God has for us. God is love, and the one who abides in love abides in God, and God abides in him. By this, love is perfected with us, so that we may have confidence in the day of judgment; because as He is, so also are we in this world. There is no fear in love; but perfect love casts out fear, because fear involves punishment, and the one who fears is not perfected in love. We love, because He first loved us. If someone says, "I love God," and hates his brother, he is a liar; for the one who does not love his brother whom he has seen, cannot love God whom he has not seen. And this commandment we have from Him, that the one who loves God should love his brother also.

The way you and I show whether we truly love God is in how we truly love others. It's not in how many times you show up for church. Neither is it in how many times you pray each day. It's not even in how much of the Bible you read or memorize. Your love for God is revealed through your love for others. It's as simple, and as hard, as that. As we saw earlier in the Romans 12 passage, we are to be "devoted to one another." Not only that, but we are also to "give preference to one another." We are to treat each other with "honor." These are not phrases that indicate a casual relationship. They reflect a heart of commitment and personal sacrifice. The gathering of followers of Jesus Christ is never to be a place where people simply meet casually every so often. It's supposed to be a spiritual house where people are committed to, devoted to, and benefiting each other with a heart of humility and service. If we can't get this right in the church, how can we expect to spread kindness in the culture at large?

It's true that we are living in a very selfish world. We are dealing with a narcissistic, me-first mentality, even in Christendom. People often come to church to cross the action off a list, to be seen, and to get a blessing. But church is supposed to be the place where you invest in others, demonstrating your love for God by how you love and are committed to the well-being of others.

When my oldest daughter was a teenager, she and I got into an argument over something I had asked her to do. Chrystal simply didn't want to do it. After much discussion, the conversation was escalating, and we were still not on the same page. When it was clear that I was not going to acquiesce nor was she going to acquiesce, Chrystal folded her arms, pouted, and walked off. That's when I asked her where she thought she was going. "I'm going to my room," she replied.

My response came quickly. "No, you're not. You're going to *my* room that I let you sleep in." After all, she had never offered to pay for any of the utilities, mortgage, or furniture. The room was technically mine. But as a teenager, she had started to believe she had more rights to it than she had. This thinking is not too different from that of many people who attend church. They walk into church thinking it is "their church," but in truth, it is God's church. They walk in thinking God is showing up for them. But God tells us to go to church to show up for Him. One way we show up for Him is in how we love and serve others.

God makes it clear throughout His Word that our vertical relationship with Him includes, inextricably, our horizontal relationship with others.

If God can't get any of His goodness, love, or blessings to flow through you to others, you have limited your own experience of His goodness, love, and blessings. It's your choice how much of God's goodness you experience. It's amazing how many people want the church in case of an emergency. There is a story told of a man who went to church one day and said, "Pastor, I need help. I can't pay my rent. I need

> ONE WAY WE SHOW UP FOR GOD IS IN HOW WE LOVE AND SERVE OTHERS. GOD MAKES IT CLEAR THROUGHOUT HIS WORD THAT OUR VERTICAL RELATIONSHIP WITH HIM INCLUDES, INEXTRICABLY, OUR HORIZONTAL RELATIONSHIP WITH OTHERS.

some financial help." The pastor asked him what church he is a part of. When the man replied he is part of the "invisible church," the pastor responded, "Well, here's some invisible money." Now, of course that is not a true story, but it gets the point across.

As a pastor for five decades now, I'll never get used to how many people view the church as a resource for themselves but would never consider investing in it or its members to be a resource for them. Unfortunately, many—if not most—of God's children are like leeches, which suck your blood and leave you nothing valuable in return. The church and its members are to do the opposite, being committed to each other in ways that enable us to impact others for good through acts of kindness that are connected to the truth (see 1 John 3:18). Instead of getting caught up in your own woes and worries, look for ways to help those in need. When you do, you will gain God's attention too. He takes notice of how you treat others. The best way to get God to move on your behalf is for Him to see you moving for the benefit of someone else.

The Motivation in Your Heart

Two men were eating lunch one day, and they both ordered a fish fillet. The waiter brought out the fish a few minutes later but brought the two fillets on the same plate. One of the fillets was huge, and the other one was small. The faster of the two men picked up the large fillet for himself and proceeded to give the smaller fillet to his friend. When he did this, his friend got upset and said, "Wait a minute, what are you doing?"

The other man responded with his own question, "What do you mean, what am I doing?"

The irritated and frustrated man replied, "You're giving me the small piece, and you kept the big piece for yourself!"

"Yeah, that's right," the man answered.

"Well, if it were me," the upset man continued, "I would have given you the big piece and kept the small piece for myself!"

The other man just smiled. He looked down at the plates. Then he said, "That's the way it worked out, so you should be happy."

Far too many times we only want to do acts of kindness if we will get something for it. Even if it's a pat on the back or a like on a social media post, we want to be sure we control the narrative around our charity. Just like the man with the fish, he was only willing to take the small piece if it came with the pride of taking the small piece. But God calls us to love without hypocrisy. We are to do acts of kindness simply because they are kind. As we devote ourselves to the needs of others, we may end up with the small fish more often than we'd like. We won't always gain notoriety for who we are and what we do. But we will gain God's attention, and that's what matters most. He notices when you live a life accented by an atmosphere of love.

Not only does God want you to be devoted to others in service and in love, but He wants you to prioritize this service. He wants you to pursue it and seek it out. He's not just calling us to be nice when someone cuts in front us in line or cuts us off on the road. He's asking us to yield to them before they do. We are to look for ways to show kindness and love to those around us. We see this calling in the passage we read earlier from Romans 12. As a reminder, it says we are to be devoted to others and show them honor while "not lagging behind in diligence, fervent in spirit, serving the Lord." *To lag behind* means "to move slowly." It's like the husband whose honey-do list takes a few years to complete: He'll get to it when he gets to it. But God doesn't tell us to show kindness and love when we get to it. If that were the case, we would never get to it. Instead, God calls us to be fervent in our spirit to serve others, because in this way we are serving the Lord. The Greek word translated as "fervent" here means "to be boiling over." God desires that we turn up the heat under our love and acts of kindness. He wants us to live passionately for His kingdom. We are to focus on the things we can contribute so that we make His service our highest priority.

When God nudges you in your spirit to do something, you are to do it right away. Don't lag behind and put it off. Don't kick the can down the road. Whatever He is asking you to do, do it. He may be working in the other person's life at that very moment and need someone from the body of Christ to show up and minister to them. As you minister to others, you are serving God. We serve God by serving others. Contributing to the needs of the saints is one way we live out our kingdom kindness calling.

But God wants us to look beyond the church walls as well. That's why the passage in Romans goes on to say that in addition to contributing to the needs of the saints, we are also to practice hospitality. The term *hospitality* is used in Scripture to refer to helping strangers. While *saints* refers to those in the body of Christ, the hospitality we are to carry out has to do with those we do not know. Whether it's through encouragement, a kind word, a kind deed, or a helpful act of service, there is a lot you can do for people you do not know. That's why we began offering Acts of Kindness cards at the church where I pastor and then expanded it to our national ministry, the Urban Alternative. These cards are used to share the gospel when a kindness is done. They aren't meant so much for people you know, but for people you don't know. When you do a random act of kindness and you ask if you can pray with that person, you are living out this idea of practicing hospitality. You are living out a hospitality of the heart.

One of the most intriguing truths concerning acts of hospitality of the heart is found in Hebrews 13. In this passage, we learn that taking care of the needs of strangers can sometimes mean that we are taking care of angels. It says, "Let love of the brethren continue. Do not neglect to show hospitality to strangers, for by this some have entertained angels without knowing it" (Hebrews 13:1–2). The Greek word translated "angels" here means "messenger." Such a messenger is a divinely assigned being who could be bringing God's answer to you. Sometimes God uses spiritual beings to meet your needs, even though you don't know they are angels.

Thus, when you practice hospitality to strangers in a responsible way, you may be engaging and assisting an angel. God has set up His kingdom to function in a cause-and-effect fashion. As you serve God through serving others, you are accessing His kingdom blessing from on high. Far too many believers are literally blocking God's blessing in their lives because they are only focusing on themselves. They are hindering God's movement on their behalf because they are trying to move only on their own behalf, without seeking ways to bless others. There must be a focus on others and their needs if you are going to go to God in prayer expecting Him to meet your needs.

Far too many of God's children are spiritual orphans. They have no family. They just bounce around from house to house with no place to land and call home. To join a church and be a part of the body of Christ is not merely to have a pew to sit in on Sunday. It is to become a part of building a community with others who share the common goal of living a life of service to those in need. No matter how large a building or how much money is spent on programs, a church is only as healthy as its people. If the environment reeks of selfishness, hypocrisy, and pride, it's a church in name only. God releases health and blessing into the church communities that make it a point to serve others in His name. Those are the churches through which He can fully express His heart of love for humanity as believers stimulate one another to love and good deeds (see Hebrews 10:24). As this happens, the church becomes a vehicle for atmospheric change, spreading kindness and love in a culture in need of hope.

FIVE

THE BOOMERANG PRINCIPLE

W e're all familiar with boomerangs. A boomerang is a device that you hurl out ahead of you, but as it spins and spins, it works its way around to come right back to you so you can catch it. The boomerang is a fun toy for kids and even adults to play with. But it is also a helpful illustration in understanding the importance of kindness in the culture. The boomerang principle, as I call it, shows up for us in Matthew 7:12, where we read,

> In everything, therefore, treat people the same way you want them to treat you, for this is the Law and the Prophets.

You've probably heard this verse referred to as the Golden Rule. It was often quoted to many of us growing up as, "Do unto others what you would have them do unto you." It's a way of approaching life that helps us live more fairly, kindly, and thoughtfully. However, you need to know how this rule really works, because if you can catch the principle behind it, it will revolutionize your experience of God.

One of the key things God wants to address in all our lives is selfishness. Have you ever noticed that no parent needs to teach their children to be selfish? No babies are ever enrolled in Selfishness 101. They come out of the womb believing that the world is all about them. And for a time, it is. Everything revolves around the baby's sleeping, eating, and diaper-changing schedule! The reason no one needs to teach babies selfishness is because selfishness is natural for humans. We all look out for the three most important people in our lives: me, myself, and I!

As we mature, though, we are supposed to learn how to become more focused on others. We are supposed to learn how to love. A quick look at the attributes of love and we can easily see that love is anything but selfish:

> Love is patient, love is kind and is not jealous; love does not brag and is not arrogant, does not act unbecomingly; it does not seek its own, is not provoked, does not take into account a wrong suffered, does not rejoice in unrighteousness, but rejoices with the truth; bears all things, believes all things, hopes all things, endures all things. Love never fails.
>
> 1 Corinthians 13:4–8

The reason God wants to rid us of our selfishness as we develop and mature is because God *is* love (see 1 John 4:7–8). God embodies true love. Love has to do with expressing care for the well-being of others. Thus, because God seeks to nurture this aspect of our humanity called love in our already-selfish souls, He has chosen to address it through this thing we call the Golden Rule. It's important to note that the verse does not say to do unto others as they are doing unto you. Rather, you are to treat others as you *want* them to treat you. It starts with you.

However you want people to treat you, treat them that way. Whatever you want boomeranging back to you, be sure to send that out in your treatment of others. In other words, what goes around comes around. God has set this up to function in this way because He wants you to experience a side of Him that you could never experience apart from the principle of the Golden Rule. He wants you to know His faithfulness and the truth of His Word in practical terms.

The Matthew passage starts with a clarifying phrase: "In everything." This is important to point out because God wants us to know that this boomerang principle doesn't only apply to certain things. This principle applies to all things. There is nothing in your life that sits outside of it. In fact, in the verses leading up to it, God lets you know that when you live by this rule, you can ask whatever you want, and it will be given to you. We read, "Ask, and it will be given to you; seek, and you will find; knock, and it will be opened to you. For everyone who asks receives, and he who seeks finds, and to him who knocks it will be opened" (Matthew 7:7–8).

God is serious about this principle. He has placed in it everything we need to fully live out our lives according to His kingdom purpose when we abide by it. He knows our humanity and our flesh. He knows we require some form of motivation. That's why the Golden Rule can also be called the Selflessness Principle. You are to treat others the way you want to be treated. You get to choose how you are treated. But that choice is not conveyed through a demand or a command. That choice is dictated by your own actions.

The problem with many people today is they want all the benefits of Christianity and of knowing Christ as their Lord and Savior, but they want these benefits with no investment on their part. Pleasing God by serving Him is not their priority. Helping someone else through acts of kindness is not their priority. Getting blessed by the Creator is their priority. But God has set up blessings to be dispensed according to His boomerang principle. If you want to be blessed, you will need to be a blessing. It's as simple as that. The boomerang only spins back to you when you prioritize loving God and loving others in your actions.

The Rules before the Golden Rule

If you choose to live a selfish life apart from God in which your choices and actions only reflect what you want, you cannot appeal to Matthew 7:7–8. These verses are connected to the principle that shows up in the Golden Rule. The reason we know that is because of the word *therefore* at the start of verse 12, "In everything, therefore . . ." *Therefore* means "in light of what was just talked about." Everything prior to verse 12 relates to this principle. We can go all the way back to the start of the chapter, where we are told not to judge. We read in verses 1–5,

> Do not judge so that you will not be judged. For in the way you judge, you will be judged; and by your standard of measure, it will be measured to you. Why do you look at the speck that is in your brother's eye, but do not notice the log that is in your own eye? Or how can you say to your brother, "Let me take the speck out of your eye," and behold, the log is in your own eye? You hypocrite, first take the log out of your own eye, and then you will see clearly to take the speck out of your brother's eye.

Judging also works with the boomerang principle. When you or I judge someone else, we open ourselves to invite others (and God) to judge us. The boomerang principle can operate on both a positive and a negative premise. This early part of Matthew 7 reveals the negative. Then verses 7–11 reveal the positive. It's the same principle of what goes around comes around, but sometimes it ushers in negativity and other times it ushers in what is positive and good. What you measure out to others will be measured back to you. Once you truly grasp this truth, it will change everything in your life.

It's interesting to note that when verse 3 addresses removing the speck from your brother's eye while you have a log in your own, it speaks of the same material, wood. A speck is a splinter or a sliver.

A splinter is painful, and if it is in the eye, it can prevent the person from seeing clearly. Thus, the splinter can represent any negative, painful scenario that hinders clear sight. Now, while you may want to come along and fix your brother's painful situation by telling him he has a problem he needs to deal with, God wants to remind you that you have a log in your own eye. Both a splinter and a log are pieces of wood. It's just that one is a lot bigger than the other. The point being that if you are trying to fix someone's problem when you yourself have an even bigger problem in the same area, you are judging and will be judged.

The Bible doesn't teach that we are not to judge. The Bible just makes the distinction that we are not to judge when we are not qualified to judge. When you judge another person for a problem or sin you yourself have, you have become hypocritical. Judging in that manner will come right back to you. Only you and God know all your issues and problems. If you don't want to be judged for the things you struggle with personally, be careful not to judge others in those things. Or it will come back to bite you.

If you have a log in your own eye, you see things even less clearly than the person with the speck. You're making a judgment based on your emotions and impressions in that moment. If you can't see the real deal, you'll fail to take into consideration all the circumstances involved in the situation. We need to remember this principle, especially during times of cultural division that are often related to politics or other values-based community discourse. So much of the vitriol in our culture comes in this area of judging others while logs remain in our own eyes. Rather than solve any issues, we've simply created a pinball-machine effect, with judgment going every which way. When you have a log in your own eye and you judge someone else, what you have measured will be measured right back. It's a spiritual principle that's gone unchanged throughout time and remains in effect today—as is evidenced on any social media site filled with comments steeped in anger and pride.

But there is also a positive side to the boomerang effect that shows up when you choose to treat others with kindness and love. Luke 6:38 gives us greater clarity on this principle:

> Give, and it will be given to you. They will pour into your lap a good measure—pressed down, shaken together, and running over. For by your standard of measure it will be measured to you in return.

Most of the time when people hear this verse, they associate it with money. Maybe it is because pastors have used it in relation to building projects or in an effort to increase giving at their churches. But the verse actually says nothing about money at all; it says "it." You get to decide what *it* is for you. For example, if you want love, then give love. If you want hope, then give hope. If you want peace, then give peace. If you want money, then give money. If you want joy, then give joy. If you want work, then give work. Whatever you want to see boomerang back to you, give that to someone else who may need it too. In this way, God is able to move you away from thinking only about yourself and expand your thinking to consider others as well. In His name, give the *it* you are wanting and you will be living out the biblical principle of the Golden Rule, and you will see how God can raise up others to give the same back to you.

When God created the world, He established this principle. In Genesis 1:11 we read, "Then God said, 'Let the earth sprout vegetation, plants yielding seed, and fruit trees on the earth bearing fruit after their kind with seed in them'; and it was so." You may not immediately see the correlation, but you will as we unpack it further. What God did to replicate His creation was to establish the natural order where everything reproduced after its kind. It's written as plural in the passage ("their kind"), but the principle holds true. Thus, if you planted apples, apples came up. Or if you planted orange seeds, orange trees came up. What's more, those orange trees did not produce pears. They produced oranges. The only way we start to deviate from this principle of replication is when scientists attempt to modify vegetation. But in God's creation, He established that whatever seed you planted, the result of that seed would be of its own kind.

Similarly, whatever seed you plant in your thoughts and actions toward others, you will receive back in its own kind. "Give, and *it* will be given to you" (emphasis added). That is straightforward. But the interesting thing comes next when we read, "They will pour into your lap . . ." The word *they* may not necessarily refer to the person to whom you gave. The word *they* could even refer to people you have never met or do not know, or even situations that are unfamiliar to you. Yet when you give to someone in His name and out of love for Him, God will touch whatever situation or individuals He needs to in order to boomerang whatever you gave back to you in a way that will bless you. It may not be identical to what you gave, but it will meet the similar need or desire in you.

Prosperity in a Kingdom Context

That's the problem with one of today's most errant theologies, known as "prosperity theology." God is not opposed to prospering you or anyone; in fact, there is a covenant of prosperity referred to in Deuteronomy 29:9. But God is opposed to people trying to use Him or portions of His principles to improve their lives apart from loving Him and seeking to help others. God is not a cosmic genie here to dispense prosperity to anyone who asks. He has set up His kingdom to function in a way that those who serve Him by serving others will receive back in kind what they give. God wants to diminish selfishness, not feed it. So while He doesn't mind helping those in need, He wants to do so in a way that enables His help to flow through you to others. That is why He demands there to be an outflow of giving to others. We read this in Acts 20:35, "In everything I showed you that by working hard in this manner you must help the weak and remember the words of the Lord Jesus, that He Himself said, 'It is more blessed to give than to receive.'"

The reason it's more blessed to give than to receive is because when you give, you also get God's attention. You've placed your own selfishness and greed to the side, focusing instead on God and His kindness to you. This is then demonstrated in how you treat others. When God knows He can use you to bless others, He will extend the flow of His provision to you at a greater level than before.

So many people struggle in their prayer life because they are asking God to do things they are not willing to do themselves. They are asking God to give them what they are not willing to give, at the level they can, to others. As a pastor, I frequently have people ask me why God is not hearing their prayers. Oftentimes, it comes down to this area of the "greatest commandments." First, are they loving God with all their heart? And second, are they willing to touch other people's lives in a way that blesses them? If the answer to either of those questions is no, then it's no wonder their prayers are hitting the ceiling. When we fail to understand God's principles and how they work, it makes the other aspects of His kingdom—things like prayer and faith—more difficult to understand. They all work in concert with each other. So many people claim that Christianity just doesn't work for them. But in reality, they have neglected to live it according to Scripture and the revealed will of God.

God wants to root out our selfishness, which goes against His nature of love, so He has set up spiritual principles for us to learn how to look beyond me, myself, and I. He instituted His boomerang principle called the Golden Rule, and under it, what you do spins back to you. So where there is a need, plant a seed. We see this in 1 Kings 17:8–16, when the widow of Zarephath is hungry and literally down to her last meal. This story illustrates the principle of the Golden Rule so clearly and vividly. Let's read it in its entirety:

Then the word of the LORD came to him, saying, "Arise, go to Zarephath, which belongs to Sidon, and stay there; behold, I have commanded a widow there to provide for you." So he arose and went to Zarephath, and when he came to the gate of the city, behold, a widow was there gathering sticks; and he called to her and said, "Please get me a little water in a jar, that I may drink." As she was going to get it, he called to her and said, "Please bring me a piece of bread in your hand." But she said, "As the LORD your God lives, I have no bread, only a handful of flour in the bowl and a little oil in the jar; and behold, I am gathering a few sticks that I may go in and prepare for me and my son, that we may eat it and die." Then Elijah said to her, "Do not fear; go, do as you have said, but make me a little bread cake from it first and bring it out to me, and afterward you may make one for yourself and for your son. For thus says the LORD God of Israel, 'The bowl of flour shall not be exhausted, nor shall the jar of oil be empty, until the day that the LORD sends rain on the face of the earth.'" So she went and did according to the word of Elijah, and she and he and her household ate for many days. The bowl of flour was not exhausted nor did the jar of oil become empty, according to the word of the LORD which He spoke through Elijah.

The widow was down to her last meal, her last handful of flour. Yet the prophet asked her for bread. He asked her for the very thing she needed most. This request tested her faith. She had to decide whether she truly believed God was trustworthy. If she did, then she would give the prophet from the little she had left. After all, he had explained that if she did, her food would not run out. She would be rewarded *in kind* for what she gave up. Because of her need, God asked her to plant a seed. But the seed had to be in her area of great need. As a result, she did not run out of food. Her kindness to the prophet boomeranged back to her, and what she received was a greater amount than what she gave up.

The same can be true for you. If you will take a moment to consider your greatest need—it could be related to work, a relationship, finances, your emotions, or many other things. Whatever it is, look for ways to be kind to others who have a similar need. Look for ways you can give hope if hope is what you need most. Look for ways you can volunteer to help a business or church if work is what you need. The Matthew 7:7 passage we looked at earlier, which says, "Ask, and it will be given to you; seek, and you will find; knock, and it will be opened to you," is written as a present imperative. An imperative is a command. God is telling you—commanding you—to keep asking, keep seeking, and keep knocking because you will get what you ask for when you tie it to His Golden Rule. This is not a suggestion. It's a command. We are to give to others, and "it" will be given back to us.

Check Your Motives

One of the condemnations in Scripture related to wrong motives is found in James 4:3, which says, "You ask and do not receive, because you ask with wrong motives, so that you may spend it on your pleasures." Connect whatever it is you are asking for to the giving of the same in blessing others, and you will get it back in kind. If it's tied only to your selfish pleasures, then it does not fall under the cause-and-effect spiritual boomerang principle of the Golden Rule. The Golden Rule attacks selfishness at its core.

Many people believe that spreading kindness in the culture is simply about checking off a list of good things done for God. Actually, kindness in the culture unleashes the power of God to work on your own behalf. It involves accessing kingdom authority for what you need. It's spiritually cyclical when it is carried out authentically.

When you give to others and bless others in God's name, you get His attention. You open yourself up to be blessed and provided for as well—in your area of greatest need. Here's a secret for living the successful spiritual life: When you go to God for something you want or need, let Him know how it will benefit others beyond you. Tell God on the front end how blessing you will bring good to others and glory to Him. When God sees that your heart is looking beyond yourself, He will allow the flow of His good provision to come to you and go through you. Then, while you are waiting on Him to supply, go ahead and bless others with acts of kindness in whatever way you can. You may not have received what you need yet, but you can do small things with what you have. God wants to see you act in faith, like the widow in Zarephath did, even if it is with a small piece of bread.

Living in light of this spiritual principle will allow you to experience more of your prayers being answered. You'll get to see God's provision in ways you had only imagined before. You'll experience this because you are now living in alignment with God's greatest commands. First John 3:22 lets us see the direct correlation between answered prayers and obedience to God: "And whatever we ask we receive from Him, because we keep His commandments and do the things that are pleasing in His sight." God answers the prayers of those who are obedient to Him, especially as related to His two greatest commands.

As you go through this book learning about what it means to show kindness to others, keep in mind that the kindness you show is not void of any benefits to you. In truth, the more kindness you show others, the more you will receive. The greater the blessing you are to others, the greater the blessings you will get in return. Let this spiritual principle shape your perspective on why it is crucial to live a life punctuated by love and kindness. When you do so in ways that bring about the expansion of God's glory and the advancement of His kingdom agenda on earth, you'll see heaven open and the favor of God come down upon you in ways that will blow your natural mind.

SIX

SECOND-MILE MINISTRY

Not too long ago, I flew to Atlanta to spend the day with Dan Cathy, one of the sons of Chick-fil-A founder S. Truett Cathy. We had a wonderful day fellowshipping, and I enjoyed getting to see behind the scenes of the Cathy family's ministry and work. They've recently invested in the development of a large-scale film production city where people can live, shop, and create movies. Many of the Marvel films have been shot there. What impressed me most as I looked at all God had guided them to do was the quality that showed up everywhere. Whether in their restaurants, their offices, or their studios, a commitment to excellence and quality is evident.

When you visit the Chick-fil-A headquarters, you will see their purpose or vision statement sitting out in front of their building. It reads, "To glorify God by being a faithful steward of all that is entrusted to us. To have a positive influence on all who come in contact with Chick-fil-A." The business is unashamedly Christian. They operate on Christian principles such as closing on Sunday, the day for attending church for most Christians. And they have one of the largest and most successful fast-food franchises in America today.

The mission statement for the restaurant will help to explain why. It says, "To be America's best quick-service restaurant at winning and keeping customers."[1]

Their four core values listed below help emphasize this goal and equip their employees to achieve it.

We're here to serve. . . .
We're better together. . . .
We are purpose-driven. . . .
We pursue what's next.[2]

The full text of the first core value reads, "**We're here to serve.** We keep the needs of Operators, their Team Members and customers at the heart of our work, doing what is best for the business and best for them." In other words, they determined to build a strong business by out-serving everyone else through teamwork, good stewardship, and innovation.

Chick-fil-A understands that the key to the expansion of an enterprise is not just having a great product but coupling that product with great service. The value of your service must be equal to or greater than the value of the product itself, or you will not sustain a loyal customer base. Nothing will make you want to leave a restaurant that offers great food quicker than a bad waiter or waitress. They can give a great restaurant a bad name because of their poor service.

A Higher Standard for God's People

Similarly, nothing can tarnish the reputation of Christians, a church, a ministry, or even Christianity in general as quickly as poor service from those who belong to Christ. And by service, I mean acts of love and kindness. To serve is to reflect God's heart. God has called each of us to ministry, whether we work in the secular world or not. He has called us to what is known as the "second-mile ministry." We read about this in Matthew 5:38–47, which says,

> You have heard that it was said, "AN EYE FOR AN EYE, AND A TOOTH FOR A TOOTH." But I say to you, do not resist an evil person; but whoever slaps you on your right cheek, turn the other to him also. If anyone wants to sue you and take your shirt, let him have your coat also. Whoever forces you to go one mile, go with him two. Give to him who asks of you, and do not turn away from him who wants to borrow from you.
>
> You have heard that it was said, "YOU SHALL LOVE YOUR NEIGHBOR and hate your enemy." But I say to you, love your enemies and pray for those who persecute you, so that you may be sons of your Father who is in heaven; for He causes His sun to rise on the evil and the good, and sends rain on the righteous and the unrighteous. For if you love those who love you, what reward do you have? Do not even the tax collectors do the same? If you greet only your brothers, what more are you doing than others? Do not even the Gentiles do the same?

When I preach sermons on this subject, the normally active and responsive congregation often sits quietly. It's easy to understand why. These verses and spiritual principles go against our natural desire to be personally satisfied and treated right. These aren't the verses you'll frequently see posted on people's social media feeds. When Jesus spoke about the kingdom culture in Matthew 5–7, there was a lot in His message that goes against our own propensities and selfish desires. One of the major points of emphasis is that kingdom people are to think and live differently from the culture in which they live.

That's why an abiding relationship with God is so important. To pull off the authentic kingdom life, you have to reach deep within and find the divinely endowed strength God gives you through the power of the Holy Spirit. In a dog-eat-dog world, loving our enemies and serving others before ourselves doesn't come naturally to any of us. These actions stem from an entirely different mindset than the normative attitude of our culture, or even our world.

In our world, if someone raises his or her voice at you, the response is often to raise yours right back. If someone messes over you, then you mess over them right back. It's the "eye for an eye" mentality that claims justice is in my own hands to pay back whatever wrong is done to me or to anyone whom I love. But the kingdom culture is different. To live in the kingdom culture, you need to look beyond what you want or need or even what seems fair. Followers of Jesus who seek to create a kingdom culture all around them adopt this mentality of going the second mile in everything they do.

Jesus has chosen and called each of us to a higher standard of living—not simply to go along with the flow of the world. He made it clear that the hallmark of His life is servanthood; He modeled it everywhere He went, even to the point of death on the cross. As followers of Jesus, we are called to both live and love like Him. We read this in Jesus' own words, spoken to His disciples shortly before He left them. He said in John 13:33–35,

> Little children, I am with you a little while longer. You will seek Me; and as I said to the Jews, now I also say to you, "Where I am going, you cannot come." A new commandment I give to you, that you love one another, even as I have loved you, that you also love one another. By this all men will know that you are My disciples, if you have love for one another.

Worship through Service

Jesus said that the way the world recognizes His true followers is by how we love and serve one another. In Matthew chapter 23 we read His words,

> Do not call anyone on earth your father; for One is your Father, He who is in heaven. Do not be called leaders; for One is your Leader,

that is, Christ. But the greatest among you shall be your servant. Whoever exalts himself shall be humbled; and whoever humbles himself shall be exalted.

Matthew 23:9–12

In kingdom culture, greatness does not come by way of titles, positions, or even possessions. It comes through service. If you are not a good servant, you are not a great person. Many of us have met successful people we would never want to spend time with because they are difficult people. They are entitled, proud people who only think of continually building their own brand or lifestyle. But spiritual success is not measured by stuff or accolades. It's measured by the ministry of service.

As a pastor, I frequently get to witness how most people come to worship *selfish*, not worship *service*. They come to church with the question of what they will get out of it and how they will benefit—or at least be entertained. Yet Jesus emphasized that if you miss the principle of servanthood in your life, you've missed one of the primary purposes and callings of salvation.

Jesus thoroughly embraced this concept of servanthood and consistently demonstrated it. One of the more memorable occasions was in the upper room, when He met with His disciples the last time before He was crucified. As His disciples sat around the table, Jesus took a towel and wrapped it around himself. He also grabbed a basin, just as a servant would have done in His day. And even though Jesus is the King of kings and Lord of lords, He modeled servanthood to His disciples by washing their feet. As He washed the grime and dust from their feet, He told them to go and do likewise. As He cleaned the muck of this world from them, He implored them to do the same for others.

Have you ever stopped to consider how dirty the basin of water must have been after Jesus washed all His disciples' feet? It must have been dark and filthy. In those days, people walked in the same streets that animals walked on, and their excrement became part of the road. People tracked all manner of filth inside with them. That is why it was common practice not just to remove a person's shoes but also to wash their feet. This helped to keep the interior rooms clean. As Jesus rinsed the rag in the increasingly gross water and rang out the towel, His own hands became exposed to the dirt over and over. In this act, Jesus demonstrated the true heart of a servant.

Above and Beyond

If there is an absence of the spirit of servanthood in a Christian or a church, there is an absence of ministry. No matter how great the sermons or how magnificent the singing or how beautiful the facilities, if the people gathering on any given Sunday are not servants in the culture at large, then they've missed the mark of Christianity. Jesus calls us to live as servants not only to those who are family or friends, but also to our enemies. In the passage we looked at in the beginning of this chapter, we see that He calls us to serve those whom we don't want to serve. As we read, "Whoever forces you to go one mile, go with him two." What that means in everyday life is to go above and beyond the requirement. Doing more than what is asked of you demonstrates servanthood. It lets the person know you are not merely crossing an obligation off a list, but you care to make an impact and a difference wherever you can.

> JESUS CALLS US TO LIVE AS SERVANTS NOT ONLY TO THOSE WHO ARE FAMILY OR FRIENDS, BUT ALSO TO OUR ENEMIES.

Keep in mind, the passage indicates situations that are not particularly pleasant. If someone "forces you" to go with them a mile, that is not a fun situation. This does not refer to times when you are hanging out with your homies. Being forced to go the first mile indicates reluctance on your part to help. A little background will help us better understand Jesus' statement. In the New Testament times, Rome was the big powerhouse. The Romans were in charge, and they often captured people and brought them under Roman rule. That means whatever the Romans wanted them to do, they had to do.

This often involved carrying things for Roman soldiers. If a Roman soldier did not want to carry his pack of goods, he could easily grab a citizen or someone who was now under Roman rule and force him to carry it instead. The Roman soldier had a sword. He wore a uniform. He held the power. When he told you to carry his goods a mile, you had no option but to comply. He was in charge and could easily force you to go a mile with him on any given day.

However, the law limited the Roman soldier to doing this for only up to a mile, to keep soldiers from overburdening the citizenry. But Jesus, when He spoke of this kingdom culture, was saying that if a Roman soldier forced you to go the full mile carrying his goods, you should go on and give him another mile for good measure. Go with him two. Servanthood should be such a dominant trait of God's kingdom people that when our liberties are infringed upon or we are imposed upon, we are to go above and beyond the requirements. The second-mile ministry spirit means we willingly give more than what is demanded, required, or asked of us.

What Jesus is establishing in the Sermon on the Mount is a mindset. It's a kingdom perspective—a worldview. He is making it clear that in the context of enemy territory or opposition, you are to serve. In fact, He goes on to say that it is easy to love those who love you. He reminds His listeners that even the tax collectors do that. Even the sinners and the secular world do that. But someone who follows Him is to love even their enemies. We are to serve even those who oppose us or want to do us harm.

Now, I understand that being a Christian would be easy if it weren't for other people. It would be easy to love others if there weren't any others to love and serve. I've heard similar comments from those in a struggling marriage. They tell me in counseling sessions that marriage wouldn't be that hard if it weren't for their spouse and their spouse's attitudes or habits. But that's the whole point. Jesus is telling us we are to serve the most difficult, love the most unlovable, and give over and beyond to those already demanding things from us. That's what going the extra mile means.

Spreading kindness in the culture isn't just about doing nice things for people behind you in a drive-through. That's easy. You'll never know or talk to those people. You'll never be offended by them or know for whom they vote! Spreading kindness is all about going the extra mile of goodness and love to those you like least. If someone offends you, all the better. Do even more kindness toward them. That will be fulfilling the calling of Jesus in your life. That will be living out what it means to truly be a disciple of Christ.

Healthy Boundaries

Now, please notice that Jesus didn't say to go three miles or even four. He's not setting you up for lifelong bondage. You are to have healthy boundaries so you are not being continually taken advantage of. Jesus called us to go the extra mile, meaning that if there is a kind act we can do for someone—even for someone we do not like—we should make sure to do it, and then graciously add some more. For example, when Jesus says to turn the other cheek, He knows you only have two cheeks. You don't keep turning it to get slapped over and over. This isn't a call to become a victim of abuse. But He is defining a kingdom mindset on servanthood. Don't do only what you have to do when asked. Do more.

If we all lived with the second-mile mindset and sought to offer more than was demanded, the atmosphere would be lifted by this love. We can have a positive impact on our society, but it isn't done by simply pointing out what everyone else is doing wrong. It is done through modeling what doing right looks like, as Jesus did.

I'm sure your home or apartment is like mine—full of appliances. These appliances have been designed with the intention of serving us. No matter what your appliance is, it is not there for the benefit of itself. It exists to cook for you, heat something for you, open a can, keep things cold, or do any number of other things. Your appliance is your servant, available to serve you at your every whim. Now, there are limitations to your appliances' service, because you don't go to your refrigerator to heat up your meat. You don't go to your juicer to make a cup of tea. In other words, your appliances serve within the scope of their capacity.

The problem with many Christians today, though, is that we are not even doing what we were designed to do. We have placed our limitations, or boundaries, too far within the scope of our purpose, limiting and restricting our usefulness in the kingdom of God. With society's me-first mindset, we've reduced all service to what someone else can do for us. But when God created you, He designed you with the intention that you would serve others. You have been given specific gifts, talents, and interests that predispose you to serving others in these areas. If you are unsure what they are, spend time praying and asking the Holy Spirit to reveal them to you. God has gifted you in such a way that you are to benefit the culture around you with His goodness through acts of kindness and love that fall in line with how He has made you. The spirit of people who are operating in a kingdom culture is made evident in how they serve. Do they only do enough to get by, or do they go the extra mile?

> GOD HAS GIFTED YOU IN SUCH A WAY THAT YOU ARE TO BENEFIT THE CULTURE AROUND YOU WITH HIS GOODNESS THROUGH ACTS OF KINDNESS AND LOVE THAT FALL IN LINE WITH HOW HE HAS MADE YOU.

Paul emphasizes the importance of this spirit in Romans 12:17–18, where we read, "Never pay back evil for evil to anyone. Respect what is right in the sight of all men. If possible, so far as it depends on you, be at peace with all men." You can't control what other people do or say. But what you can control is your response to them. Paul urges us in this passage to live with a heart of kindness and love. When we do, we will not pay back evil for evil. We will respect what is right in the sight of all men. And we will, as far as it depends on us, live peacefully with all people. There are enough Christians remaining today to dramatically influence our culture for good if we choose to live by biblical principles of kindness. This election season, or any election season, does not have to be a dominant influence on our lives, minds, conversations, or interactions with others. We do not have to stoop to the level of society, but rather, we can rise above it.

How We Treat Our Enemies

I recently released a dramatic series on the life of David through a popular app online, and as I went back through his life studying how he conducted himself, one of the things that stood out to me most was how David treated Saul with kindness. Time and time again, David had the opportunity to oust his enemy from power by force. Yet David never paid back Saul's evil with evil. Even when he had the opportunity to kill Saul, David chose to live by God's principles. He said he would not touch God's anointed (see 1 Samuel 26:1–12).

That doesn't mean David hung around to be hurt by Saul. He fled when he had to. But he also didn't illegitimately take matters into his own hands. He left room for the wrath of God. Eventually, Saul committed suicide, which opened the door for David to be king. Paul tells us to always leave room for God to act, and we do this by choosing kindness. We read in Romans 12:19–21,

Never take your own revenge, beloved, but leave room for the wrath of God, for it is written, "VENGEANCE IS MINE, I WILL REPAY," says the Lord. "BUT IF YOUR ENEMY IS HUNGRY, FEED HIM, AND IF HE IS THIRSTY, GIVE HIM A DRINK; FOR IN SO DOING YOU WILL HEAP BURNING COALS ON HIS HEAD." Do not be overcome by evil, but overcome evil with good.

If you've never seen God intervene on your behalf, you may want to check your own kindness meter. How kind and loving are you to those who offend you or oppose you? God doesn't usually barge in to carry out His wrath on those who treat you unfairly. We are told we must "leave room" for God to deal with our enemies. Leave room by choosing kindness and going the second mile when someone forces you to go one.

We see this in the life of Joseph as well. He was treated unfairly by his brothers, thrown into slavery, then accused falsely of rape. Joseph ended up in jail due to others' poor treatment of him. Yet when his brothers came to him years later in great need of food, Joseph let them know that he forgave them, that what they had intended for evil in his life, God had turned around for good (see Genesis 50:20). God had used their mess to move Joseph up in the world and to save the lives of many, including theirs.

If you grasp this concept, it will be life-changing. By simply choosing kindness and love when others mistreat you, you leave room for God to bless you and use the situation for good. But if you retaliate through your own words, bad attitudes, or poor conduct, God allows you to do just that—retaliate—and only that. He doesn't rectify the situation, because, in your pride, you thought you could handle it on your own. Trusting God's principles of love and kindness increases His ability to work things out for good in your life (see Romans 8:28). God doesn't promise to work all things out for good unconditionally. He promises to do so only when you are loving Him by loving others and living according to the calling He has placed on your life. One of the major components of this calling, of course, is in your willingness to go the second mile in what you think, say, and do in His name for those around you.

I urge you to give it a try. Test God on this truth. As you do, you'll come to experience Him in a whole new way as you see Him show up for you in ways only He can.

SEVEN

KINDNESS TO THE LEAST

As previously mentioned, summer in Texas means heat, heat, and more heat. The sun is out longer and seems to burn brighter. If you come to Texas in the summer, or if you live here, you know what it's like to sweat. You know what it's like to fan yourself. And if you spend time in the heat, you know what it's like to smell. In other words, it quickly becomes apparent that the sun has affected you if you spend any amount of time in it.

Similarly, it should be quickly apparent that the Son of God has affected each of us as well. There should be evidence of spending time with the Son, Jesus Christ. When you commit your life to Him as His kingdom follower, you need to spend so much time in His presence that He affects you in ways others can identify. If that's not the case, then maybe you are not spending enough time with Jesus. Just as the Texas sun will have an effect on you if you are in its light, the Son of God will have an effect on you when you are in His light.

As we are seeing through our time in this book, when you do not positively touch the lives of others with God's love, you are revealing to others that you have not been sufficiently affected by the Son of God. We know this because Jesus came to demonstrate the love of God to each of us, and He wants to use you to demonstrate His love to others in word and deed.

Far too often, we confuse religion with what it means to be spiritual. No matter how many church services you go to, Bible studies you participate in, or pews you flip while you get your praise on, if other people's lives are not benefiting from the time you've spent with the Son, He has not rubbed off on you. Your love of God shows when you love others with visible and verbal demonstrations of kindness. To recap a bit of what we have learned so far, one of the ways you demonstrate love to others is by meeting the needs of your neighbor. Your neighbor can be defined as the person whose need you see and feel led to meet, and whose need you have the capacity to meet. Showing love means addressing a need in a biblically legitimate way while doing so tied to God's name, based on His Word, and for His glory.

The more time you spend with Jesus, the more sensitive you will become to others and their needs. The less time you spend with Jesus, the less sensitive you become to others and their needs. Jesus has established His body to live as His hands and feet in a world full of needs. We are placed here to fulfill this high calling of kindness in the culture within our spheres of influence. And while doing so to those you know may come naturally, it is often more difficult to show kindness to strangers.

Kindness to Strangers Is Kindness to Jesus

Jesus knew this would be more difficult for us to do. That's why, when talking to His disciples, He emphasized our need to open our eyes to those around us, especially those whom we do not know. What He said is recorded for us in Matthew 25:31–40. We read,

> But when the Son of Man comes in His glory, and all the angels with Him, then He will sit on His glorious throne. All the nations will be gathered before Him; and He will separate them from one another,

as the shepherd separates the sheep from the goats; and He will put the sheep on His right, and the goats on the left.

Then the King will say to those on His right, "Come, you who are blessed of My Father, inherit the kingdom prepared for you from the foundation of the world. For I was hungry, and you gave Me something to eat; I was thirsty, and you gave Me something to drink; I was a stranger, and you invited Me in; naked, and you clothed Me; I was sick, and you visited Me; I was in prison, and you came to Me." Then the righteous will answer Him, "Lord, when did we see You hungry, and feed You, or thirsty, and give You something to drink? And when did we see You a stranger, and invite You in, or naked, and clothe You? When did we see You sick, or in prison, and come to You?" The King will answer and say to them, "Truly I say to you, to the extent that you did it to one of these brothers of Mine, even the least of them, you did it to Me."

Many of us are familiar with this passage. And sometimes, when we get too familiar with a passage, we neglect to process it and apply it in our lives. But we must apply this passage if we are to live as faithful kingdom followers of Christ. It details a key component of the Christian life.

Here Jesus is letting us know that whatever we do to or for another human being, in His name, we are doing to or for Him. He's helping us to see the correlation between serving others and serving Him, the direct link between loving others and loving Jesus.

Have you ever gotten a gift for your birthday or Christmas that was something you didn't want? Not only that, but you couldn't even find a good use for the present? Yet, because it was a gift, you did not feel comfortable getting rid of it either. So you put it in a closet, the garage, or the attic and hoped the person who gave it never asked about it. It was a wasted gift.

Unfortunately, a lot of Christians give Jesus gifts He has no use for—things He does not want or need, whether it be volunteering or writing a song. Yet because we feel compelled to give to Jesus, we give Him that which makes no difference to Him or anyone else. It can be different for each person what the various gifts are, but unless they are gifts that Jesus asks for and are given with a heart of love, they do not amount to much in His kingdom economy. But Jesus made it clear what kinds of gifts He likes. He wants us to give the gift of demonstrating His love to others through verbal and visible acts of kindness.

If someone is in need and you can meet that need, Jesus wants you to do that. That's what it means to spread kindness in the culture. And that is the gift Jesus wants. If a person is thirsty, give them something to drink. If someone needs a tangible item that you can assist them in getting, then help them out. If someone is disabled and can't move their furniture, and you have the use of your limbs, then help move their furniture. Whether it's a meal, an encouraging message, or mowing a lawn, give the gift of your tangible help. When you do this in Jesus' name, it becomes a valuable gift to Jesus himself, especially when it is combined with prayer, encouragement, or a gospel witness, depending on the spiritual condition of the person.

> **THE LOVE CHRIST HAS CALLED US TO SHOW IS A LOVE THAT DOESN'T EXPECT ANYTHING IN RETURN. WHEN YOU SERVE SOMEONE ELSE WITH THIS HEART AND INTENTION, YOU ARE TRULY DEMONSTRATING WHAT IT MEANS TO LOVE GOD.**

But instead of thinking of acts of kindness as gifts to Jesus, we often look at them as a form of leverage. After all, we live in a world where everyone wants to cut a deal. If you do this for me, I'll do that for you. That has become the norm and is called "transactional kindness." But this so-called "kindness" is not true kingdom kindness at all. The love Christ has called us to show is a love that doesn't expect anything in return. When you serve someone else with this heart and intention, you are truly demonstrating what it means to love God.

This reminds me of a short conversation two men had. One man was standing next to another and said, "Sir, excuse me, but you smell like roses." He made the comment because it is not common for a man to smell like roses.

The other man smiled, shrugged his shoulders, and replied, "Yes, that's probably true. I'm a florist, and I spend all day in the florist shop."

This is another way of illustrating that where you spend your time shows up on you. If you choose to spend your time with Jesus, His love and kindness will rub off on you. But if all you focus on is yourself instead of drawing close to Him, then it won't. Jesus says that whatever you do to the least of these, you have done to Him. That's the kind of love Jesus wants to rub off on you so that you reflect His aroma of goodness and kindness wherever you go, permeating your spheres of influence.

Jesus has not hidden what we should do to serve Him and bless Him. We are called to take care of others in His name. We are called to love others, especially the least of these, through acts of kindness in His name. There exists a direct correlation between love for God and love for others, particularly those who have nothing to offer you in return. The more God sees you helping those who cannot return your help, the more you will experience His presence made manifest in your life.

Now, I understand that you have your own problems, your own struggles, debts, and inconveniences—you may even need help from someone else. But one of the ways you can help yourself is by helping others. As we saw in the last chapter, by serving others you open the door for God to respond to you and bless you in your need. And as we just read in the Matthew 25 passage, those who have shown their love for Jesus by caring for the least of these are invited to "come, you who are blessed of My Father, inherit the kingdom prepared for you from the foundation of the world" (v. 34).

On the other hand, Jesus has strong words for those who ignored the needs of others—and who in doing so failed to show love for

Him. He tells them to "depart" from Him. We read in Matthew 25:41–46,

> Then He will also say to those on His left, "Depart from Me, accursed ones, into the eternal fire which has been prepared for the devil and his angels; for I was hungry, and you gave Me nothing to eat; I was thirsty, and you gave Me nothing to drink; I was a stranger, and you did not invite Me in; naked, and you did not clothe Me; sick, and in prison, and you did not visit Me." Then they themselves also will answer, "Lord, when did we see You hungry, or thirsty, or a stranger, or naked, or sick, or in prison, and did not take care of You?" Then He will answer them, "Truly I say to you, to the extent that you did not do it to one of the least of these, you did not do it to Me." These will go away into eternal punishment, but the righteous into eternal life.

Your relationship with Jesus will always show up in your actions, in how you treat others and care for their needs. I do want to clarify before we go further that you are not expected to meet every need. You can't. I can't. But those needs that you see and that God gives you a heart's desire to meet and the capacity to meet, those are the ones you are to meet. Do not quench the Holy Spirit's nudging in your heart. When God calls your number to show up and serve Him by meeting someone else's needs, do it.

Giving with the Right Mindset

Luke 14:11–15 explains the mindset we are to have when contributing to the needs of others:

> For everyone who exalts himself will be humbled, and he who humbles himself will be exalted.
> And He also went on to say to the one who had invited Him, "When you give a luncheon or a dinner, do not invite your friends

or your brothers or your relatives or rich neighbors, otherwise they may also invite you in return and that will be your repayment. But when you give a reception, invite the poor, the crippled, the lame, the blind, and you will be blessed, since they do not have the means to repay you; for you will be repaid at the resurrection of the righteous."

When one of those who were reclining at the table with Him heard this, he said to Him, "Blessed is everyone who will eat bread in the kingdom of God!"

The bottom line in this passage is this: Invite those who have nothing to give you in return. If you have a dinner party and invite only your peeps—your comfortable crew—then you are extending your hospitality to those who can repay you. They may not repay you in kind, but you know they will be there when you need them. Jesus explains that this type of hospitality has its reward built in transactionally. Rather, He says, invite "the poor, the crippled, the lame, the blind," and others who similarly can't give you anything in return. When you do this, you will be blessed by God himself. It's up to you to decide whose blessing you want—your friends' or God's.

When you give to others in God's name and you do it for their benefit, without expecting them to repay you in any way, God records this act of kindness. Jesus tells us there will be rewards for us in eternity for the good works we do in His name. But if you demand repayment in this life from whomever you blessed—whether through a return favor or anything else—then you've gotten your reward already. You can forget about the eternal reward. Demonstrating your love for God in tangible acts of service will open heaven's blessing later on.

Emphasizing this point in another way, Jesus demonstrated to His disciples how, and whom, to love and serve. We read in Matthew 18:1–7,

At that time the disciples came to Jesus and said, "Who then is greatest in the kingdom of heaven?" And He called a child to Himself and set him before them, and said, "Truly I say to you, unless you are converted and become like children, you will not enter the kingdom of heaven. Whoever then humbles himself as this child, he is the greatest in the kingdom of heaven. And whoever receives one such child in My name receives Me; but whoever causes one of these little ones who believe in Me to stumble, it would be better for him to have a heavy millstone hung around his neck, and to be drowned in the depth of the sea.

"Woe to the world because of its stumbling blocks! For it is inevitable that stumbling blocks come; but woe to that man through whom the stumbling block comes!"

Jesus tells us clearly that the greatest in the kingdom of God is the person who humbles himself as a child. Not only that, but to be great in God's eyes is to receive children in Christ's name. In the culture at that time, children were the "least of these" in many ways. They were often left unattended or forced to work to help the family survive. Jesus knew that children were often overlooked and discarded by adults, which is why elsewhere in Scripture we read that He rebuked His disciples for turning away kids. It says in Mark 10:13–16,

And they were bringing children to Him so that He might touch them; but the disciples rebuked them. But when Jesus saw this, He was indignant and said to them, "Permit the children to come to Me; do not hinder them; for the kingdom of God belongs to such as these. Truly I say to you, whoever does not receive the kingdom of God like a child will not enter it at all." And He took them in His arms and began blessing them, laying His hands on them.

Jesus not only taught in word but also in deed the value of children. He demonstrated what James 1:22 says, "But prove yourselves doers of the word, and not merely hearers who delude themselves." The disciples had tried to push the children away from Jesus. But Jesus not only invited them to come near—He also blessed them.

Nurturing Our Children

In America today, we don't typically put our children to work in the field to help provide the family's food. But we do often turn them loose with video games or digital devices to keep them out of our hair. We're living in a day of some of the highest-ever levels of child neglect. But Jesus tells us what matters most in His kingdom. He tells us that if we want to be great in God's eyes, we not only need to become humble like a child but also must welcome the humble—the discarded, the ignored, the set aside—into our lives. We need to bless them as He took the time to do. Christians, and not the government, should be leading the way in bringing kindness, civility, and charity to the culture.

Jesus also gave a firm warning in the passage we looked at earlier, letting it be known that if you mess with a kid, you are messing with Him. Kids are totally dependent on adults for many things. That also makes them vulnerable. Knowing this, Jesus harshly condemned any poor treatment of kids. He let us know that we will never become great in His kingdom as long as we fail to treat the most vulnerable with kindness and love. We are to responsibly invite them into our lives as Jesus invited the children over to Him to bless them.

Where I pastor, in every month that has a fifth Sunday we have what is called "Family Church." This is where we encourage families to worship together. Much of the service is led by our children and youth departments. We close the regular Sunday school classes and have everyone in the main sanctuary for this special time. It happens only four times a year, but you would be surprised how frustrated some people get over our having

> **JESUS LET US KNOW THAT WE WILL NEVER BECOME GREAT IN HIS KINGDOM AS LONG AS WE FAIL TO TREAT THE MOST VULNERABLE WITH KINDNESS AND LOVE.**

these special Sunday services. I admit, the sanctuary is noisier, and the service doesn't follow the typical program. But we are to welcome and bless children as Jesus did, because He values them.

We are to value children as well and are responsible for their growth and development. We are to take an active role in this. To illustrate, there was a pastor who wanted to show off his garden to one of his church members whom he knew would never bring his children to service. So as he was going around his garden with the man and showing him the things he was growing, he asked, "Why don't you ever bring your kids to church?"

The man replied, "Well, I don't want to force them. I want them to grow up and make their own decisions."

That's when the pastor got to a section of his garden that he had purposefully allowed to be overgrown with weeds. There were weeds everywhere, choking out the life of the plants he had put in a few months earlier. The vegetables were rotting, shrunken, and ugly. They just couldn't grow with the weeds draining the nutrients and moisture from the soil. That's when the man asked the pastor, "Why did you let this part of your garden turn out like this?"

"Well," the pastor replied, "I just wanted the vegetation to decide for itself what should grow there."

Parents and adults have been given the responsibility to nurture and nourish the growth and development of children. This is what it means to serve Christ. Doing acts of kindness for other adults who are established and can somehow repay you is nice, but it is not what God considers great. Greatness in the spiritual kingdom means serving the least of all, who are often children. Children can't do a whole lot for you in return for what you do for them. The blind can't do a whole lot for you when you help them, nor can the lame. But when you serve the least of these, in Christ's name, you are filling a storehouse of reward in heaven. You are elevating yourself in God's eyes and according to His standards. Later on, when you need something from God, He will be able to look into your account and see the good works you have accumulated in His name.

I spend a lot of my time preaching to large audiences in Dallas and around the nation. I've even preached before a million men on the National Mall in Washington, DC. But when God looks down and sees me preaching His Word to thousands of people, He doesn't credit me with greatness for that, doesn't turn to Jesus and say, "Hey, look at Tony Evans! Wow!" Rather, greatness shows up in the acts most people never see. It's the kindness to those who can do nothing in return—that's what catches God's eye. Never overestimate yourself based on the things you do in public. God looks at your heart and examines your motives. Are you helping those who cannot help you in return? Are you welcoming children in His name to bless them? Are you showing up in ways most people will never even know, and are you bringing the good news of Jesus Christ with you? When you model your life after Jesus Christ, you will live a life of true greatness.

It's All about Jesus

There's an insightful fictional story about the donkey who carried Jesus on Palm Sunday. It's an illustration that helps shed light on how and where we are to find our true greatness. On Palm Sunday, the donkey walked down the road with his head held high. He had Jesus on his back, and people were waving and cheering everywhere. Palm branches were being placed before him so that he didn't have to walk on the rough road. The donkey quickly became very proud. After all, who else carried the Messiah? But the next day when the donkey got up and walked down that same street, no one noticed him. No one waved any branches. No one cheered. He stepped on the hard, uncomfortable road.

When he got home, he asked his mom what had happened. Why was everyone cheering one day but absolutely ignoring him the next?

That's when he learned the truth. His mom replied, "Son, without Jesus, you're just a donkey."

We can all learn from this story. Without Jesus, we are nothing. It is His power and will that work in us to carry out the acts of love and kindness we do. Serving Jesus with a humble heart keeps us in step on His path. It keeps us in line with His purpose. It can even elevate us to a position of true greatness in His kingdom. With Jesus, the way up the ladder is down. Service to the "least of these," even when it involves just a cup of cold water (see Matthew 10:42), is what matters most.

EIGHT

HELPING LAME PEOPLE LEAP

Many of us have in our home things that have been broken and not repaired. Something that might have been shattered, or possibly a ceramic decoration with a piece chipped off. We have things waiting to be glued, bound, repainted, or otherwise fixed. Sometimes, depending on how busy we are or how uninterested we may be in fixing them, these things pile up. After a while, this mini hospital of restoration items can appear overwhelming. It isn't until we decide to work on them that they will be transformed from broken to fixed.

But this scenario doesn't happen only with things. Lives can become broken too. When lives get broken or shattered and there seems to be no way to repair them, people can feel hopeless. Whether you are looking at your own life, a loved one's, or the life of someone else you know, it might seem like the situation can't be rectified.

Sometimes this can happen with the physical body. Other times it can happen with dreams, goals, or lost opportunities. This can lead to a person living a life full of regrets and disappointments. When we find ourselves or our loved ones in situations like this, the best most people are hoping for is to try to get by. The light is gone from their eyes, and they are simply trying to make it to the next day. When hope for the future wanes, enjoyment of today similarly dissipates.

In Acts 3, we read about someone in a similar situation. His difficulty related to his body, and due to his physical limitations, he undoubtedly suffered emotional, relational, and financial loss as well. We can see from the passage that he was lame from his mother's womb. Both his ankles and his feet were afflicted, and he had never walked. We also discover that he was over forty years old (Acts 4:22). He had known only perpetual dependency his whole life and had to rely on others to carry him around so he could beg. He hadn't been able to run and play with friends as a child or keep a job as an adult.

It's hard to man up if you can't even stand up. Yet this was the predicament of the lame man. No doubt he lived with shame, pain, and emotional defeat. His whole life was based on the charity and kindness of others. Whether his stomach would remain empty or be filled each day depended on the goodness in other people's hearts.

This man's dependence was not an event. It was a lifestyle. He lived in the midst of a pain that neither he nor anyone around him could address or fix. The Acts 3 account tells us that every day people would carry him to the temple gate called Beautiful so he could ask for alms—the cash he needed to survive.

An interesting thing about the gate called Beautiful was that it was a gold-plated gate. It took upwards of twenty men to open and close it. This huge gate served as the main entrance for the prayer meetings held during that time. We read that both Peter and John had come at the ninth hour to pray. The ninth hour (three in the afternoon) would have been the last of the prayer times during the day, with the other two being held at nine in the morning and noon.

It's important to remember that at this time, the temple was the central location for people to gather and worship or pray. The Christian church had only been established a short time before this, so Christians still went to the Jewish temple for prayer. The last prayer session of the day was the largest and most attended because that was the time the sacrifices were performed. Thousands of people would flock to the service to take part in the blessing of prayer and sacrifice. This explains why the lame man would be there during this specific prayer time, if not all day long. It would be his best opportunity to gain charitable gifts from the crowd.

Another interesting observation is that this man's main place to get help was the temple, where he knew people would be most inclined to give him cash. Yet even though many were able to give to him, they were never able to change his destiny. In other words, the temple made it convenient to be a beggar while doing little for his overall circumstances. This is important to point out because at times, our acts of kindness may only be prolonging a difficult situation rather than offering a spiritual solution. It can become somewhat easy to meet temporal needs of those who are in a bind, but God has called us to much more. God has called us to live kind and charitable lives that impact people for eternity. Peter and John knew this greater calling when they heard the beggar's plea; they knew they were to respond at a higher level than simply dropping coins in a cup, as we will soon see.

Peter and John had gone to the temple for prayer. Throughout the New Testament, and particularly in the book of Acts, there is a huge emphasis on prayer. Prayer is designed to allow people to contact heaven to communicate about what needs to be addressed on earth. Prayer has the ability to connect the spiritual realm to the physical realm. That's why Jesus called the temple "a house of prayer" (Matthew 21:13, Mark 11:17). Prayer is foundational to the spiritual life. Jesus never referred to the temple as "a house of preaching" or "a house of singing." The temple was called "a house of prayer" because prayer rests as a central tenet of what God created the church to be. The ability to contact heaven to bring about a positive transformational impact on earth is essential.

Peter and John saw the man as they went to pray. Undoubtedly, you have also seen people who beg. They may not sit at the entrances of churches in our culture today, but they will often sit or stand along busy roads or intersections. They come to ask for money. Sometimes their affliction is noticeable. They may be crippled or missing a limb. Other times their affliction is not as identifiable, but they still hold up a sign begging for help. It usually says something about their being hungry and just wanting a meal for the day. When Peter and John saw the man who was hungry by the gate to the temple, they didn't look away. Instead, they fixed their gaze on him. They stopped. They noticed him. They paused their plans and paid attention to the man in need.

Peter and John's example is a good one for all of us who want to live lives that positively impact those around us. Peter and John didn't look the other way when they passed by the lame man. Rather, they stopped and looked directly at him. What's more, they asked him to look at them. We read, "But Peter, along with John, fixed his gaze on him and said, 'Look at us!' And he began to give them his attention, expecting to receive something from them" (Acts 3:4–5).

It's no wonder the lame man looked at Peter and John when they asked him to. He quickly gave them his attention because he expected them to give him something. If you were a beggar on a street corner and someone rolled down their window, motioning you over to them, wouldn't you expect to get something? That's only natural. Your hopes would be raised. Your thoughts might move toward what you would get to eat soon with the money they were about to give. It's like the feeling you get when you open a birthday card, expecting a gift inside. You don't even bother to read the card. You just shake it, seeing what falls out—cash or a check.

But nothing fell out of the envelope for the beggar this time. Peter and John didn't place a single coin in his cup. Imagine his disappointment when Peter said, "I do not possess silver and gold." Whatever faint smile he might have had was gone as fast as Peter could say the words. Peter let the lame man know he wasn't asking for his attention so that he could give him money. He didn't want to participate in the temple welfare system or give him a handout so he could merely survive another day. No, Peter wanted to give him something more.

Kingdom Authority

Peter and John didn't have much money, but what they did have was delegated kingdom authority. They had been given heaven's authority to speak into the crisis the lame man faced and change the course of his destiny. The wonderful part of this story is that Peter and John did not have anything more than we do as believers and followers of Jesus Christ. You and I have been delegated as kingdom ambassadors representing heaven's interests and will in history on earth.

The problem is that far too few of us make any use of it. Far too few of us spend our lives spreading not only acts of kindness to address temporal needs but also actions rooted in kindness and authority to change lives for eternity. Each of us has been given by God the authority and right, when carried out according to His divine will, to make tomorrow better than yesterday. We have the kingdom authority rooted in Jesus Christ to alter futures so they outpace the past. As we carry out kingdom authority through acts of kindness based in prayer and in Jesus' name, we can advance God's kingdom agenda on earth.

> EACH OF US HAS BEEN GIVEN BY GOD THE AUTHORITY AND RIGHT, WHEN CARRIED OUT ACCORDING TO HIS DIVINE WILL, TO MAKE TOMORROW BETTER THAN YESTERDAY.

When Jesus was on earth, He told his disciples in Luke 9:1 that He was giving them kingdom authority: "And He called the twelve together, and gave them power and authority over all the demons and to heal diseases." What's more, when Jesus rose from the dead, He signaled access to kingdom authority in His name as we carry out His will on earth.

And Jesus came up and spoke to them, saying, "All authority has been given to Me in heaven and on earth. Go therefore and make disciples of all the nations, baptizing them in the name of the Father and the Son and the Holy Spirit, teaching them to observe all that I commanded you; and lo, I am with you always, even to the end of the age."

Matthew 28:18–20

God gave access to kingdom authority to us, His disciples, through the ascended Lord Jesus Christ. Jesus sits on the right-hand side of the Father because that side is always indicative of strength. Jesus is positioned there to execute God's will in history through His authorized kingdom agents. Jesus' authorized agents are those believers who have been delegated the kingdom authority to act on Christ's behalf in light of His physical absence on earth. Through the indwelling power of the Holy Spirit, we are to execute Jesus' will on earth. This can only be done through the authority of Christ and in His name.

What's important to understand is that all believers do not share equal authority or execute equal spiritual power. Ephesians 3:20 gives us a glimpse as to why: "Now to Him who is able to do far more abundantly beyond all that we ask or think, according to the power that works within us." In other words, a believer only receives the "far more" abundant work of God in his or her life "according to the power that works" within him or her. The abundance of authority and work is tied to the level of kingdom power able to be executed. If you do not have great power, you cannot do as much as those who have more. God has made His power available to all of us through an abiding faith and relationship with Jesus Christ (John 15). Yet not everyone takes advantage of this offer. Therefore, God has chosen only to do through you, His authorized kingdom agent, that which you have gained access through His power to do. It is up to you to cultivate your relationship with Jesus Christ in order to gain greater access to God's kingdom power in you.

In Jesus' Name

When you drive to town, you may see a police officer also driving on the road. If you go to a concert or a large event, you'll see a police officer directing traffic. When that officer holds up his or her hand, people stop walking or driving in that direction. The police officer's hands do not contain special forces. The reason people stop driving or walking across the street is due to the authority granted to the police officer by the law. The officer serves as a representative of the government who is duly authorized to control traffic. It's not the hand that holds the power. It is the authority represented by the hand that does the work.

If you or I were to go out in a street and try to direct traffic, it is unlikely we would find any success. As the cars continued to zoom past us, we would quickly realize just how unauthorized we are. Similarly, just because you and I go to church does not automatically guarantee kingdom authority at a level that will enable us to drastically improve someone else's life—or even our own. Authority to carry out kingdom-sized acts of kindness comes tied to the name of Jesus Christ. It was in Jesus' name that Peter and John accessed the authority they needed to help the lame man. It was their connection to His name that gave them the power to pull off the miraculous feat. The full text of Acts 3:6 says, "But Peter said, 'I do not possess silver and gold, but what I do have I give to you: In the name of Jesus Christ the Nazarene—walk!'"

Peter acknowledged the kingdom authority he had through a relational connection to Jesus Christ. He said, "But what I do have I give to you," which lets us know that this kingdom power to change lives through acts of kindness isn't tied only to Jesus' name. It is also tied to your connection to Jesus himself.

For example, if you were to go to 1600 Pennsylvania Avenue and walk up to the guard facility and say, "Tony Evans in Dallas sent me here to talk to the president," you wouldn't get very far. Even if you called on my name many times and demanded to be let in, they would merely escort you off the premises. You would soon find out that my name holds no weight at the White House. But if you were to come to the church where I pastor, Oak Cliff Bible Fellowship, and use my name attached to my wishes to be carried out, you would gain the authority you needed to do it. My name carries weight at the church where I pastor because it is tied to my role and relationships there. In other words, knowing and using a name successfully is tied to the authority of that person and your relationship with them when you use it.

A lot of Christians want to use Jesus' name, but when there is no relationship to Him as a person and as their Savior and Lord, they come to find out their words do not carry His authority. Jesus' name is not a magic word to be used on your every whim. Just because you know the name of Jesus does not mean you have been authorized to use it. Only when you abide in Christ according to the Scriptures will you gain access to the authority of Jesus' name. This holds true for individuals, families, churches, and communities.

Performing acts of kindness is good. And performing them with the spiritual authority and power of Jesus will enable you to potentially transform someone's life. But that spiritual authority and power are actualized only through the abiding fellowship of Christ in you.

A story in Acts 19 demonstrates this key aspect of Christ and His authority, with relationship to His name. In this passage, we read that Paul has been casting out demons left and right. These demons begin to flee whenever Paul shows up and speaks. As you might imagine, a good deal of power and clout will follow anyone who has this ability. As people see what Paul is doing, some of them want to do it too. They don't want to do it to help others, though. Instead, they want to benefit from the clout and recognition. They want what Paul has so that they might receive applause and other material gain. Let's read this story in Acts 19:11–17:

God was performing extraordinary miracles by the hands of Paul, so that handkerchiefs or aprons were even carried from his body to the sick, and the diseases left them and the evil spirits went out. But also some of the Jewish exorcists, who went from place to place, attempted to name over those who had the evil spirits the name of the Lord Jesus, saying, "I adjure you by Jesus whom Paul preaches." Seven sons of one Sceva, a Jewish chief priest, were doing this. And the evil spirit answered and said to them, "I recognize Jesus, and I know about Paul, but who are you?" And the man, in whom was the evil spirit, leaped on them and subdued all of them and overpowered them, so that they fled out of that house naked and wounded. This became known to all, both Jews and Greeks, who lived in Ephesus; and fear fell upon them all and the name of the Lord Jesus was being magnified.

Basically, the demons told the seven sons of Sceva that they knew Jesus and they knew Paul, but they had no idea who they were. The name, when its authority was not tied to the individuals invoking it, proved useless. In fact, the demon not only refused to come out, but it also jumped on the men and beat them up, leaving them to flee, naked and wounded. Using Jesus' name only goes as far as your personal connection to His name, underneath His lordship and authority in your life. Jesus is looking for people who will be agents of transformation in a culture gone crazy. It is our job to help change people's lives for good, not only in the moment but for eternity. But Jesus will only sanction the authorization of His divine authority for those He knows as His own. Your power to transform lives is tied to your personal relationship with Jesus Christ and level of submission to His authority.

In other words, prayer is not enough. Jesus' name is not enough. Your kingdom authority is actualized through an abiding presence of Christ made manifest in the Holy Spirit's work in your life. Peter and John had this power, and with it, they healed the lame man. After telling the man to walk, Peter reached down and "seizing him by the right hand, he raised him up; and immediately his feet and his ankles were strengthened. With a leap he stood upright and began to walk; and he entered the temple with them, walking and leaping and praising God" (Acts 3:7–8).

Jesus Acts through Us

You and I are the hands and feet of Jesus. Peter didn't just talk to the man. He didn't just pray for the man. Peter reached out and touched the man. He grabbed his hand and lifted the lame man up. The actions Jesus desires to do from heaven are done through people here on earth. We are to be actively involved in helping people. Merely telling someone you are praying for them is not maximizing kingdom authority or fully expressing kingdom kindness. God has equipped you to touch them and change their situation through your relationship with Jesus Christ.

Prayer is powerful. But prayer without action is only one part. Similarly, action without prayer is only one part. There's got to be motion to the prayers you pray. That is walking by faith. If there is no movement to the prayer, there is no execution of the heavenly power on earth. All through Scripture you see demonstrations of this. There were many times when God would not move until the people or person first moved in response to what He asked.

> MERELY TELLING SOMEONE YOU ARE PRAYING FOR THEM IS NOT MAXIMIZING KINGDOM AUTHORITY OR FULLY EXPRESSING KINGDOM KINDNESS. GOD HAS EQUIPPED YOU TO TOUCH THEM AND CHANGE THEIR SITUATION THROUGH YOUR RELATIONSHIP WITH JESUS CHRIST.

God told Moses at the Red Sea to hold up the rod. The Red Sea did not open until Moses did as God told him to (Exodus 14:21). He told the priests to put their feet in the river so that the waters would separate and Israel could cross (Joshua 3:13). He gave the command to move the stone before He raised Martha's brother Lazarus from the grave (John 11:39). In other words, you can pray all day long, but until your life aligns with your lips, your prayers will just be words. If God has told you to take some sort of action to address a situation, walking by faith means doing it. When Peter reached down and seized the man by the hand, the lame man's legs strengthened and he was able to stand. He didn't have to go to a doctor. He didn't require crutches. The strength of his ankles began to form when Peter grabbed him. In fact, the Scripture we read says he jumped up. He didn't just barely stand up like an old man might do. He leapt. What's more, he continued to leap as he praised God for allowing him to experience the supernatural in the natural realm. When the authorized agents of God mixed prayer with action, this lame man's life was transformed.

The Power of Kingdom Transformation

God can turn things around on a dime. That's how powerful He is. No matter how long the problem has been there, how deep it has gotten, or how much damage it has caused, it can be fixed. When the right kingdom agent of God combines the right prayer with the right action, an act of kindness or charity can lead to true life transformation. What we need today are men and women who aren't just looking for government charity but rather kingdom transformation. No one has to let their past control their future. As kingdom ambassadors from God's throne, we have the ability to change lives for good and for God's glory.

When this is done, it will not just be one person's life that will be changed, but when others hear about it, they will be changed as well. We read in Acts 4:4 about the impact Peter and John's kingdom authority in the lame man's life and their explanations of the gospel had on the community: "But many of those who had heard the message believed; and the number of the men came to be about five thousand." Five thousand—and that did not count women and children. Peter and John were leading people to Christ by combining words of faith with works of faith.

Peter and John used the miracle of the lame man's healing as a platform for sharing God's love and His salvation with others (Acts 3:11–26). In the Old Testament, David did the same thing when he showed kindness in God's name to Mephibosheth, the lame son of Jonathan who had nothing to offer him in return (2 Samuel 9). We are to do the same. Not only are we to perform acts of kindness to make this world a better place, but we are to tap into the kingdom authority of God and use these opportunities to share the gospel. Any sinner can do a good thing. But a good work is more than a good thing. A good work always glorifies God.

When you package prayer, acts of kindness, and the sharing of the gospel together, you become a kingdom ambassador, seeking to advance the kingdom of God on earth. It is my hope that the communities and churches in our land will become so full of kingdom kindness ambassadors that people will marvel at the power of God. Our nation ought to be swept with people who are looking for opportunities to serve God by helping others in His name. There are a lot of people suffering today who need the help of the Lord. They need a healing hand. They need a hope-filled word. God has called each of us to be His hands and feet, to open our hearts and our eyes to His work in people's lives. When we do that, we become instruments of God's transforming love. It is this perspective that makes kingdom kindness different from secular acts of charity.

NINE

RICH IN GOD'S WORK

Many fast-food restaurants offer the option of increasing the size of your order. Some call it "super-sizing." Before you pay for and receive your order, you'll often be asked to make it bigger than what you had originally asked for. I'll admit, it's hard to say no when you are hungry. You might have pulled up to the drive-through thinking you would just get a regular meal, but by the time you drive off you have super-sized the whole deal.

When you trusted Jesus Christ as your Savior, you received eternal life. Everyone who places faith in the finished work of Jesus Christ for their personal salvation gains access to this free gift. But God wants to make you an offer for something more. God is offering to super-size your experience with Him. He doesn't want you to settle for basic Christianity or a spiritual Happy Meal life. He wants to offer you much more beyond that, based on His Word.

Salvation through Jesus Christ guarantees you entrance into heaven when you die. Christians realize that and count on it. Yet what most Christians do not realize is that being saved is no guarantee for a super-sized spiritual life. All who are saved do not get the full expression of God's reality operating to and through them. That comes by virtue of your alignment under and fellowship with God.

Now, some people may say that they don't need a super-sized spiritual life. They may feel satisfied with a Happy Meal. That may be what Paul was facing when he penned the letter to Timothy, his mentee in the faith. Paul encouraged Timothy to teach his congregants what would benefit them the most.

At the time when Paul wrote to Timothy, there were three general classes of people—much like today. There were the poor, the middle class, and the rich. The lowest group among the poor were known as the slave class. If you were a slave, you generally didn't own anything and spent your days eking out just enough to allow you to eat and survive. You didn't have many changes of clothes. Everything you did was aimed at survival.

The next group in society was the middle class. In biblical times, the middle class had their own dwelling place. They could own a home and even some possessions. They had more than one change of clothes. They did more than just think about how to get their next meal. They had more time for exploring life and engaging in it.

The third group were the rich. This group of people lived in abundance. They didn't have to eke out a living just to eat. Nor did they need to work to cover basic wants or to have a little extra to spend on the weekends. The rich lived in luxurious homes, with their domestic needs attended to by the poor and middle class. They had extra money, extra clothing, and large premises. They never had to worry about their next meal or a stack of bills.

These three groups composed society at the time Paul wrote to Timothy. Knowing these three distinct groups gives us context for Paul's statement in 1 Timothy 6:7–8, which says,

> For we have brought nothing into the world, so we cannot take anything out of it either. If we have food and covering, with these we shall be content.

Paul began by encouraging contentment. You have to start there. Paul wanted people to realize that if they had food and clothing, they should not complain. Complaining is a manifestation of discontentment, which reflects a heart of ungratefulness. Paul wanted Timothy, and those Timothy taught, to know that having the basics in life should produce a spirit of contentment rooted in gratitude.

Paul tried to make sure, before even starting to talk about what it means to be rich and to desire the super-sized spiritual life, that there was an understanding of contentment. *Contentment* means "to be at ease where you are, to be satisfied with what you have." It doesn't mean you can't hope for more or work for more or pray for more. But it does mean you are fine with and grateful for what you have right now, while you wait for something to change.

A person who is prone to complaining though they have ample food and clothes has an entitled heart, not a contented one. Gratitude produces contentment. Ingratitude produces entitlement. In America, the line for distinguishing poverty typically runs about $20,000 or less per year. The government has determined that to earn less than that means you cannot cover your basic needs like food, shelter, and medical costs. That's when the government will step in with assistance. But if you make more than that, up to about $100,000 a year in income, you are considered the middle class. Depending on family size and how many people are in a household, those are the general delineations. As of 2023, the average annual income in America is $71,000. Yet a recent Gallup poll found that most Americans believe the minimum average income in order for a family to "get by" is $85,000 per year.[1]

These are the figures for America. But if you look at the world, to be considered in the top 10 percent of wage earners globally, you need to make $122,000 per year. The average global income is about $23,000 per year, and the average income of the poorer half of the global population is $3,920.[2] When you look at global standards, or if you have ever traveled to or visited impoverished areas, you can quickly understand that even the poor in America earn more than those worldwide. Even many of the poor in America have access to food and water, whether through government assistance or charity, as well as a place to live. This reality ought to produce a heart of gratitude for what you have because there are billions of people worldwide who barely earn enough to survive.

If you don't have to wonder how you are going to get from point A to point B because you have a vehicle and enough money to fuel it, you need to reevaluate any complaining you do. You should be content. If you have a closet to put your clothes in and get to choose what you are going to wear, then contentment ought to be your main setting. I'm not saying you shouldn't want to earn more, do better, or achieve success. What I am saying, and what Paul is saying in the passage we are looking at, is if you have food and clothes, you should be content. You should not live in a grumbling mood.

But after Paul looked at what it means to be content and how contentment should serve as our starting point for spiritual growth, he went on to tell Timothy about how to go about wanting more. We read this in 1 Timothy 6:17–19, which says,

> Instruct those who are rich in this present world not to be conceited or to fix their hope on the uncertainty of riches, but on God, who richly supplies us with all things to enjoy. Instruct them to do good, to be rich in good works, to be generous and ready to share, storing up for themselves the treasure of a good foundation for the future, so that they may take hold of that which is life indeed.

Keep in mind, this comes on the heels of Paul's writing in verses 10–11, "For the love of money is a root of all sorts of evil, and some by longing for it have wandered away from the faith and pierced themselves with many griefs. But flee from these things, you man of God, and pursue righteousness, godliness, faith, love, perseverance and gentleness." Here Paul is seeking to differentiate between money and loving money. He never said that *money* is the root of all evil. Rather, he said *the love of money* is a root of evil. He wants to establish this up front because he's about to give a message on how to super-size your spiritual life.

God is not against people being rich. God is not against people being blessed. All through the Bible, we read about those who are rich. In fact, Solomon was one of the richest people of his time. Abraham was also rich. Job was rich. What's more, it was God who supplied their riches by blessing them. We read in 1 Samuel 2:7, "The LORD makes poor and rich; He brings low, He also exalts." God can build you up. He can also allow an economic collapse to tear you down. All of these things are in God's hands.

The book of Proverbs has many verses on how to obtain riches or wealth in slow and steady ways. There is much written against get-rich-quick schemes. The Bible promotes a lifestyle of hard work with an eye on earnings. Proverbs 10:22 says, "It is the blessing of the LORD that makes rich, and He adds no sorrow to it." Scripture doesn't reveal a condemnation against the rich. There are many who fit in the category of abundance. But Scripture does warn that riches come with potential side effects.

Beware the Sin of Pride

One of those potential side effects of wealth is conceit, or pride. The more a person acquires, the greater the possibility for wrong thinking to seep in. It can become easier to think more highly of yourself than you ought. You can become self-absorbed and consider yourself better than other people. In the old days, we'd refer to that as "stuck up and sadity." But there is no basis for arrogance when you realize that God himself chooses to bless. If it weren't for Him, the rich would not be rich. That's why Paul emphasizes this warning when writing to Timothy. He wants Timothy to guide his flock in such a way that they know the warnings on great wealth.

I was watching a football game the other day when a commercial came on talking about how a certain medicine could help relieve certain symptoms. Images of healthy, happy people filled the screen. But for the majority of the commercial, the narrator listed the ways side effects from this medication could harm you. In fact, he finally mentioned the medication can sometimes even be fatal. I'm sure you've seen similar ads. By law, drug manufacturers are required to tell the potential side effects. God wants you to know that becoming rich also has potential side effects, one of which is conceit.

There's nothing worse than a stuck-up saint, someone who feels that because they are blessed, everyone else must be doing something wrong to be facing hardships. They believe that the goodness in their lives is tied to their choices and actions, rather than to the grace of God. They have forgotten who they are and how far God has brought them. Paul warned of this happening and urged believers not to set their hope on the "uncertainty of riches." Riches can come and go, here today and gone tomorrow. An accident, illness, death, or anything you own that breaks can quickly teach you how fragile and fleeting money is. When something goes sideways, upsetting your plan, it can change your financial status quickly. Circumstances have a way of reminding us that all good things that come to us are by God's grace. James 1:17 says,

> Every good thing given and every perfect gift is from above, coming down from the Father of lights, with whom there is no variation or shifting shadow.

It's important to remember who your Source is. When you recognize God as your Source, you can remain confident even when things change. You can also keep yourself from pride when you are blessed. Pride is one of the inhibitors of sharing your blessings with others. For believers to spread kindness in the culture, we must root out all pride and ownership thinking. We are kingdom stewards put here on earth to shepherd what's been given to us in such a way that it brings God glory and good to other people.

Trusting in your riches is putting all your marbles in your own money basket. That's dangerous. God is opposed to pride. If you choose to be proud, God will often allow something to humble you and remind you that He is your Source. We read how God feels about pride over and over in Scripture:

> The fear of the LORD is to hate evil;
> Pride and arrogance and the evil way
> And the perverted mouth, I hate.
>
> Proverbs 8:13

> But He gives a greater grace. Therefore it says, "GOD IS OPPOSED TO THE PROUD, BUT GIVES GRACE TO THE HUMBLE."
>
> James 4:6

> Everyone who is proud in heart is an abomination to the LORD;
> Assuredly, he will not be unpunished.
>
> Proverbs 16:5

> There are six things which the LORD hates,
> Yes, seven which are an abomination to Him:
> Haughty eyes, a lying tongue,
> And hands that shed innocent blood,
> A heart that devises wicked plans,
> Feet that run rapidly to evil,
> A false witness who utters lies,
> And one who spreads strife among brothers.
>
> Proverbs 6:16–19

> Pride goes before destruction,
> And a haughty spirit before stumbling.
>
> Proverbs 16:18

The Lord of hosts has planned it, to defile the pride of all beauty,
To despise all the honored of the earth.

Isaiah 23:9

Riches and money are not the problem. Pride is the problem. Riches and excess money, however, can contribute to the problem of pride, which is why Paul warns us against this. Focusing your mind and your heart on how to serve others with the blessings God has given to you, through acts of kindness, generosity, or charity, also helps keep your heart in check when it comes to pride. Psalm 62:10 reminds us, "If riches increase, do not set your heart upon them."

> **GOD WANTS YOU TO ENJOY WHAT HE HAS GIVEN YOU. HE JUST DOESN'T WANT WHAT HE HAS GIVEN YOU TO STEAL YOUR THOUGHTS AWAY FROM HIM.**

Our heart must always be set on God. In other words, don't let the stuff you have snatch your love and devotion for God. Don't let it grab your affections.

Instead, set your hope on God, who richly supplies all you need. God wants you to enjoy what He has given you. He just doesn't want what He has given you to steal your thoughts away from Him. In short, He doesn't want His gifts to become an idol.

The Proper Mindset toward Blessings

This chapter isn't meant to make you feel guilty for what you have or for being blessed. Neither is what Paul wrote in Scripture. It's intended to warn you of the potential side effects, or dangers, of focusing on your wealth more than God. If you have received wealth legitimately and are using it legitimately, then you can enjoy it legitimately. Ecclesiastes 5:18–20 emphasizes this:

> Here is what I have seen to be good and fitting: to eat, to drink and enjoy oneself in all one's labor in which he toils under the sun

during the few years of his life which God has given him; for this is his reward. Furthermore, as for every man to whom God has given riches and wealth, He has also empowered him to eat from them and to receive his reward and rejoice in his labor; this is the gift of God. For he will not often consider the years of his life, because God keeps him occupied with the gladness of his heart.

You are to enjoy the gifts and blessings God has given to you. There's no need to apologize about it or let other people make you feel bad about legitimately accumulating those gifts and blessings. God knows that life comes with difficulties and pain. He knows there are hard times. That's one of the reasons He's given us good things to enjoy when we can. And once you have learned how to enjoy your blessings without letting them dominate your life as an idol, you are ready to benefit even more through a life of goodness and kindness. God wants to bless you as you bless others. We are called to be rich in good works. Thus, the richer God makes you in money, the richer you ought to be in good works. If your money is going up but your good works are going down, something is wrong. You have somehow created a spiritual disconnect.

If you want to be blessed but are unwilling to be a blessing because you are so focused on yourself, you have drifted from God. When you are close to God, His generosity toward you will be reflected in your generosity to others. As a reminder, a good work is a divinely authorized activity that benefits someone in need and for which you do not expect a return and for which God gets the glory. God must be the motivating factor for it to be a good work. As Matthew 5:16 says,

Let your light shine before men in such a way that they may see your good works, and glorify your Father who is in heaven.

To glorify means "to praise, advertise, proclaim, or put something on display." Each act of kindness you do needs to be intentional, with the effect bringing glory to God. When you don't attach it to God and His provision as the Source in all our lives, then it's just a good thing. Good things may help in the moment but don't impact the eternal destiny of the person you helped or cultivate his or her present relationship with God. What's more, good things have no impact on your own relationship with God. A good work that glorifies God, on the other hand, draws His attention toward you. It calls in the request to super-size your spiritual life. It brings God pleasure. As Hebrews 13:16 says, "And do not neglect doing good and sharing, for with such sacrifices God is pleased."

Treasure in Heaven

If you want to make God smile, be rich in good works. Be rich in *God's* work. To do this means establishing boundaries in your own life on what you do for yourself or spend on yourself, but it will also open the floodgates of heaven for God to send more. The more you roll up your sleeves and invest your time, talents, and treasures in others for God's glory, the more you will discover His goodness flowing to you. A good work is not just a check or online donation. While those things are good and helpful, God is asking you to invest all of your blessings in blessing others. That includes you. Your time. Your gifts. Your abilities. Your hard work. It may mean having to change clothes from a dress shirt to a T-shirt to meet a material need. It may mean changing your plans to accommodate someone else who is in need. It may mean showing up for the sick, homebound, or at-risk. It may mean using a particular skill or connection to benefit someone. Whatever the case, you are called to do good works, and more often than not, they are not something you can just mail in. Good works include your involvement and engagement with others.

We are to set up our lives so we can be available if someone is in need and to arrange our finances so we have surplus when God sends someone our way. You can start by volunteering your time somewhere that meets the needs of others. Or by coming up with a way to help an elderly person or even someone in your family who may need help. Whatever it is, when it is tied to God's name it will bring Him glory. God will take notice and He will respond to you with His favor. Ephesians 4:28 says, "He who steals must steal no longer; but rather he must labor, performing with his own hands what is good, so that he will have something to share with one who has need."

> **WE ARE TO SET UP OUR LIVES SO WE CAN BE AVAILABLE IF SOMEONE IS IN NEED, AND TO ARRANGE OUR FINANCES SO WE HAVE SURPLUS WHEN GOD SENDS SOMEONE OUR WAY.**

The purpose of work is to provide for yourself, to serve the location, industry, or customers where you work, but also to provide something to share with others who have need. When you do this, you store up for yourself treasures in heaven while releasing a greater experience of God here on earth. As we read earlier in 1 Timothy 6:18–19,

> Instruct them to do good, to be rich in good works, to be generous and ready to share, storing up for themselves the treasure of a good foundation for the future, so that they may take hold of that which is life indeed.

Being rich in God's work through good works allows each of us to store up treasure for ourselves in eternity and to "take hold of that which is life indeed." That's where this concept of super-sizing the spiritual life comes in. When you become active in doing good works, you are front-loading a storage facility in heaven. It always amazes me that despite the size of houses today, there are still storage facilities going up everywhere. Apparently, humanity has a propensity for accumulating stuff. Knowing this, God urges us to store up that which will not rot or decay. He urges us to store up what we can use forever in eternity. It's literally saving for the future, when God plans to unveil the eternal vastness of His kindness to His people (Ephesians 2:6–7).

Most of us know what it means to save for the future in this life. We have retirement accounts or investments. Many parents save for their kids' college educations. Our future-oriented thinking informs our choices today. God is asking us to think further into the future, past what we see and know now. He's asking us to store up what will last forever. We do this through good works. When you reach heaven, God will give you what you have stored up. If your eternal storage unit is empty, then you have no treasures in heaven.

Storing things in heaven also enables you to take better hold of your life today. As we have seen, one of the reasons many people are not experiencing more of God is because their storage unit in eternity is empty. They have been concerned only about themselves, so when they ask God to super-size their experience of Him right now, He checks out their balance and finds it lacking. To truly maximize and enjoy a super-sized spiritual life, you must live with a future orientation. You must make your choices based on what you hope for in the future as well as on your current needs. Because when you go to God to withdraw something for the present life from your heavenly storage, He's going to look inside. If He opens it and finds nothing, then that's what you may get.

We are all going to face difficult times in our lives, times when we need God to intervene. We will face seasons when even money won't be able to solve the problem. We're going to need divine intervention and assistance. Everyone faces those times when riches can't buy you out of it, friends can't deliver you from it, and your own mind can't figure a way through it. Those are the times when we will frequently turn to God and ask for His mercy and provision. But oftentimes, what goes around comes around when it has to do with receiving spiritual solutions for earthly issues.

There is a wonderful story found in Acts 9:36–42 that illustrates this for us:

> Now in Joppa there was a disciple named Tabitha (which translated in Greek is called Dorcas); this woman was abounding with deeds of kindness and charity which she continually did. And it happened at that time that she fell sick and died; and when they had washed her body, they laid it in an upper room. Since Lydda was near Joppa, the disciples, having heard that Peter was there, sent two men to him, imploring him, "Do not delay in coming to us." So Peter arose and went with them. When he arrived, they brought him into the upper room; and all the widows stood beside him, weeping and showing all the tunics and garments that Dorcas used to make while she was with them. But Peter sent them all out and knelt down and prayed, and turning to the body, he said, "Tabitha, arise." And she opened her eyes, and when she saw Peter, she sat up. And he gave her his hand and raised her up; and calling the saints and widows, he presented her alive. It became known all over Joppa, and many believed in the Lord.

Tabitha was a woman abounding in good works. She would have been a Kindness in the Culture ambassador in her town. Charity and acts of kindness flowed freely from her. We could say she was rich in good works. But what is interesting is that when Tabitha fell sick and died, Peter was called upon to come and help out. Knowing the need and knowing her reputation, Peter went quickly. When he arrived, everyone started showing him the wonderful things Tabitha had done for others. The women grieving around her were women she had helped.

At this time, Peter opted to send everyone out so he could kneel down and pray. Doing so, he asked for the dead woman to arise. And while Peter didn't perform the miracle himself—God did— Tabitha did respond to his request, and she got up. She was alive. Tabitha, who had done so many acts of kindness and goodness for others, got her own miracle. Her business of abounding in good works to help those in need came back to bless her in her moment of crisis.

Friend, when you are in a situation that your skills can't fix, or your checkbook can't fix, you need to ask yourself whether there has been enough goodness in your own life for God to give you the miracle you need most. Will He raise you back up because He knows you will be a blessing to others? Now, it's true that on earth everyone will die. Tabitha did eventually die and remain dead. Even the righteous and saints die. So this isn't a formula for eternal life on earth. But it is a good example of the power of God in times when we need Him most.

If you are to maximize your spiritual potential—to super-size your life—you must be wealthy in good works. That doesn't mean a random act of kindness when it's convenient. To be abundantly wealthy in good works means that kindness is your lifestyle. Whenever and wherever you have the opportunity to serve someone else, do it. Do not ignore the nudging of the Holy Spirit inside you. God is watching, and He notices when you do good works for His glory.

One of the biggest problems in our nation today is that we have too many people climbing the ladder of success only to get to the top and find out it was leaning against the wrong wall. It doesn't matter how many rungs are in your ladder or how high it goes. It matters that you lean it against the correct wall. If you spend all your time climbing ladders to nowhere, then you'll get there. It's absolutely critical that you place your ladder on the wall of God's love, climbing ever closer to His heart with each step. As you do this, His blessings will pour down on you, and consequently, pour down on others through you.

Spreading kindness in the culture is about changing our culture for good and replacing chaos with compassion. It's about uplifting the atmosphere from one of negativity and vitriol to one of encouragement and hope. But in addition to all that, it's about elevating your own spiritual life and experience with God. This movement is full circle. As each of us begins to participate more and more in sharing acts and words of kindness in our realms of influence, we will also be ushering in a revival of God's presence in our churches and in our land.

CONCLUSION

Kingdom Cultural Impact

The prophet Zechariah reminded us how a culture can be unkind and unjust. Expressing justice is a way of demonstrating kindness in the culture. Yet because society and culture are often driven by ungodly systems, structures, and people, this gives rise to a contagious virus of meanness. As this contagion spreads, God removes His hand of blessing, provision, and peace from a land. When this happens, the land becomes desolate. *Desolate* can refer to a number of things. It is not only talking about the ground and the ability to grow food. Desolation also affects trade, commerce, and even societal health and engagement. We see this time and time again in Scripture, but one of the places it is most directly expressed is in Zechariah 7:8–14. It says,

> Then the word of the LORD came to Zechariah saying, "Thus has the LORD of hosts said, 'Dispense true justice and practice kindness and compassion each to his brother; and do not oppress the widow or the orphan, the stranger or the poor; and do not devise evil in your hearts against one another.' But they refused to pay attention and turned a stubborn shoulder and stopped their ears from hearing. They made their hearts like flint so that they could not hear the law and the words which the LORD of hosts had sent by His Spirit

through the former prophets; therefore great wrath came from the Lord of hosts. And just as He called and they would not listen, so they called and I would not listen," says the Lord of hosts; "but I scattered them with a storm wind among all the nations whom they have not known. Thus the land is desolated behind them so that no one went back and forth, for they made the pleasant land desolate."

The goal of the church is to bring God's perspective to the culture. It is to take God's kingdom perspective beyond the four walls we meet within each Sunday. We do this through good works. Matthew 5:16 says, "Let your light shine before men in such a way that they may see your good works, and glorify your Father who is in heaven." God wants us to go public with our kindness. Letting our light shine is done through acts of kindness and love. God doesn't just want private kindness, personal kindness, or even ecclesiastical kindness. He wants kindness in the culture.

While we are called to be kind in the church, kind in our families, and kind in our relationships, kindness in the culture takes God's glory public. In this way, we are ambassadors of God's kingdom everywhere we go. God desires that the portrait of who He is, His image reflected in and through His body, be put on display in all places. He wants to be made visible and has created and called each of us to take part in this great mission.

Our deteriorating culture does not have time for secret agent Christians. When it comes to kindness and love, God wants you and me to demonstrate these attributes in the public square. As Galatians 6:10 puts it, "So then, while we have opportunity, let us do good to all people." When Scripture says we are to do good to "all people," it means just that: *all* people. Even the people you don't know, might not care for, and don't agree with. Kindness is not a limited commodity. Kindness is to be a way of life.

That's why we've developed a Kindness in the Culture campaign, which is detailed in appendix B. It's a campaign to motivate Christians to set a new tone in the public arena. There are so many ways you can show kindness, whether it's in helping a homeless or elderly person, providing a meal for someone in need, sending a gift to someone who is struggling, visiting the sick, opening the door at a store or restaurant, picking up something someone dropped, offering a delivery driver a bottle of water, or any number of things. When you see and feel a need and know you have the ability to meet that need, God is asking you to step up and respond with a kind action.

What's more, when you do meet a need, ask the person if you can pray for them. Your prayer doesn't need to be fancy or long. But when you pray, you are visibly and verbally demonstrating your dependence on God and glorifying Him. After all, they may know God, and this could draw them closer to Him. Or they might not know God personally, and this could be a step toward their getting to know Him. Your prayer opens the spiritual door for the Holy Spirit to do His work. Don't be nervous about praying for someone. Most people for whom you do an act of kindness will let you pray for them, and most will also feel comforted by that prayer and the care you show in taking the time to pray.

Then, if you are able, share the gospel. The good news of the gospel is the most important part because that is the ultimate manifestation of God's kindness (Titus 3:4–5). However, there isn't always the opportunity to do that. That's why we've put a link to the gospel presentation on the kindness cards so people can watch it online. In this way, your acts of kindness are the work of evangelism as you go about your everyday lives. Our good works should always lead to the good word of the gospel. If and when enough Christians commit to doing at least one act of kindness a week, we will be helping to transform our culture.

Together, we can develop a movement of kindness and love. We can counteract the meanness and vitriol that have become far too normal in our nation today. It's time for Christians individually and the church collectively to take the lead in developing and spreading the impact and influence of kindness in the culture.

ACKNOWLEDGMENTS

I want to thank my friends at Baker Publishing Group for their interest and partnership in bringing my thoughts, study, and words to print on this valuable subject. I particularly want to thank Andy McGuire for leading the charge on this manuscript with Baker Publishing Group. It's been a pleasure working with Andy to see this through to print. I also want to publicly thank Sharon Hodge and Hannah Ahlfield. In addition, my appreciation goes out to Heather Hair for her skills and insights in writing and collaboration on this manuscript.

APPENDIX A
GOING DEEPER THEOLOGICALLY—
Questions and Answers on Kindness

QUESTION: How can we reconcile the kindness of God toward all creation with the reality of God's wrath toward sinners?

ANSWER: Paul says in Romans 11 that God is both kind and severe. There's the goodness of God and yet, there is also the holiness and justice of God. Both are equally true.

The good news is that God can allow one of His attributes to react to another of His attributes. That's why when we repent, God will relate to us with mercy rather than judgment because we responded to the merciful side of His character. God's perfections cannot be compromised. But we can adjust which perfections we are relating to and benefiting from by meeting the conditions He has established.

QUESTION: How is the cross a symbol for God's response to the unkindness of the world?

ANSWER: The cross of Jesus Christ was God's response to sin. God's response to sin was invoked to set up an appropriate penalty so He could offer forgiveness. God wanted to offer the whole world forgiveness by extracting the price for sin from His own Son, Jesus Christ—a kind act that keeps Him from having to do that to us. Thus, He carried out His wrath within His own Trinitarian family. That's kindness and love. That's the sacrificial kindness that offers us forgiveness. Whenever someone offers you forgiveness at no cost to you, that's the highest form of love.

QUESTION: Paul tells us in Romans 2:4 that it is God's kindness that calls us to repentance. We often forget this in our approach to sin and think that fear and anger are better motivations to bring about repentance. Why is God's way of kindness the best approach?

ANSWER: One of the ways God draws us to repentance is through His kindness. When we get ahold of how good He has been by not giving us the consequences that we deserve and by lessening the repercussions of mistakes we've made and sins we've committed, that ought to wake us up to want to respond to that kindness with gratitude, with repentance, and with commitment. We should remember this in how we treat others, choosing kindness rather than hate or judgment.

QUESTION: Galatians 5:22 reminds us that kindness is a fruit of the Spirit. How does the Spirit work within us to develop this fruit so that we are kind Christians in the midst of an unkind world?

ANSWER: We're told in Galatians 5 to "walk by the Spirit." That means to operate spiritually, to seek to please the Lord with your decisions. When you do this, you are operating in the realm of the Spirit. When you make the choice, based on God's Word, to operate in the realm of the Spirit, then the Spirit's work is activated in your life to produce the fruit or the result of that decision. While God won't decide for you, once you choose to operate spiritually and ask the Holy Spirit to impart to you what you need in this area of kindness, the Spirit will help you and is able to produce the results of that decision.

QUESTION: Even though the church is called to be a community of kindness, this is often not the witness we offer the world and is not necessarily the virtue that outsiders know us for. Why do you think the church, which has been shown God's kindness, is known less for its kindness and more for its fighting and controversies?

ANSWER: One of the reasons people do not see kindness in the church is that the church is often not spiritual. The church has become so secular in its thinking that it reflects the vitriol in the culture. As a result, the church has become a poor witness to the world. Because we are not walking in the Spirit—thinking spiritually while relating to the Word of God as we should and asking God's presence to inform the atmosphere in which we operate—our wrong thinking spills into our actions, and people don't get a good testimony from the church on the issues we face today.

Even if we're biblically correct in what we believe or profess, the way we carry it out or share it is often unbiblical because our manner can be mean-spirited. It can even be hateful, divisive, and proud. Instead, we've got to ask God to not only give us the truth but balance this truth with love. So we can be "speaking the truth in love" (Ephesians 4:15). When love is missing, the truth becomes hard to hear.

QUESTION: One of the main ways we spread kindness in the culture is through good works. What distinguishes good works from good deeds?

ANSWER: What are good works in Scripture? Good works are beneficial actions that you do for another in God's name. You're helping a person who needs help, and you're attaching God to the assistance that you are giving. Then it becomes an even greater work when you share the gospel, because that brings eternal benefit to the temporal assistance you are giving.

In that combination, people can see and feel the love of God—not just hear about it—through the kind acts we demonstrate to one another and to others who need to see the love of God in tangible form.

KINDNESS IN THE CULTURE CAMPAIGN

Be a part of the dynamic new initiative by Dr. Tony Evans that is spreading an atmosphere of hope across our nation. Replace hurtful speech with helpful speech. Choose honor over hate. DO what God says: "Do not be overcome by evil, but overcome evil with good" (Romans 12:21).

If we each do our part, we can create a collective ripple, reaching further than we ever could on our own.

How It Works

It's easy. Just open your eyes and your heart to perceive how God leads you to do one act of kindness a week. If you want to do more, all the better! But when you do it, be sure to ask the recipient if you can pray with them. Also ask if you can present the gospel to them. They may not say yes, but that's okay. Just smile and give them a card. On the card is a QR code they can use to watch a gospel presentation some other time. Everyone is different, and the person you talk to may be introverted or private, so don't be offended if they don't want you to share the gospel. Just leave the card and leave room for the Holy Spirit to continue the work you started.

Share the Gospel

We all know that we're supposed to share the gospel with others, and we genuinely want to. But sometimes sharing the good news of Jesus Christ can be intimidating. We've put together these resources to help you do your part in taking the gospel to a world in need.

What Are Acts of Kindness?

Acts of kindness can be anything from offering to carry groceries for someone who is struggling (maybe an elderly person or a young mom) to bringing a cup of coffee to a coworker, helping a neighbor, taking someone lunch, tipping more than standard, offering to help someone who looks lost, holding the door open, letting someone in line ahead of you, to simply being intentional about what you say and seeking to encourage someone who is down.

There are so many ways we can all be more kind. These are just a few ideas, and we know you'll come up with some great ways too.

Spread Kindness

You can get kindness cards from the ministry by contacting us directly, but if you want to have the kindness cards **customized** to your local entity, moms' group, men's group, women's group, prayer group, church, or organization, simply email us at kindness@tonyevans .org and we'll reach out to you. That way you can include the **name** of your organization or group (and if it's a church, your worship times), or any other information on the back of the card to let people in your community know where they can get together with more awesome and super-kind people like you.

To discover more, go to TonyEvans.org/Kindness.

HOW TO SHARE THE GOSPEL (BRIEF)

In a time when many dismiss the gospel message, it is our responsibility to make sure people have a chance to hear the good news. You and I need to be prepared to tell others about the hope that is within us. How do we do that? In this appendix, I give a brief overview of sharing the gospel as well as a link and QR code at the end where you can hear me share this information with you personally on video. In the next appendix, I provide you with the complete Romans Road gospel presentation.

When you want to share the gospel with someone, I would recommend that you begin with a question. You might ask, "How do you think a person gets to heaven?" or "Would you like to be sure you are going to heaven?" By asking a question and listening to their answer, you earn the right to share your thoughts. Since many Christians do not feel very confident about how to share the gospel, I've put together a simple approach that is based on three verses from Romans.

First, Romans 3:23 tells us that "all have sinned." Most people recognize that they are sinners and have done and said things that are wrong. The truth of this verse should be obvious to all, since this is the universal situation of each of us. It's the diagnosis for our spiritual disease. We all struggle with the reality of a sin problem and what to do about it.

Second, Romans 5:8 offers us the great hope that "while we were yet sinners, Christ died for us." The good news is that God loves sinners. He did not leave us in our sinful state but has offered us a way out. As a demonstration of God's love for us, He gave us His Son, Jesus Christ, who died on the cross as a payment for our sin. Christ is our substitution, the One who takes our place. The perfect One, Jesus, takes upon himself the punishment that we deserved. His love wipes out our debt and frees us from our guilt.

Third, Romans 4:4–5 makes clear that our salvation comes through God's gift, through the sacrifice Christ made on our behalf. It is not because of our efforts to do the right thing or become better people. None of our works are good enough to earn us an invitation to heaven. Our salvation isn't a reward for our goodness, but it is a gift that God offers to those who believe in Jesus for the forgiveness of sins and the free gift of eternal life. God credits the perfection of Jesus to our account; His righteousness pays off our debt.

You can finish by sharing a couple of other Scriptures that echo the message of those in Romans that we just discussed. Most people have heard John 3:16, which speaks of the greatness of God's love—so great that He gave His only Son so that we could have eternal life with Him. And 2 Corinthians 5:21 tells us that Christ is the One who was without sin but was made to be sin for us so that in Him we might become "the righteousness of God." This is the good news that changes hearts and changes lives. We should be bold in proclaiming it to those who need to hear.

To view the video, go to TonyEvans.org/ShareTheGospel
or scan the QR code below.

THE ROMANS ROAD GOSPEL PRESENTATION

I've included this section with two purposes in mind. First, for those who have never been acquainted with the basic foundations of the Christian faith, I want to present them clearly. Second, for those who are Christians, I want to teach you a powerful and complete way to share your faith with others.

The outline we'll use is not original. I did not discover it; I simply enlarged upon it. However, I've found it simple to remember and easy to use. It's called the Romans Road. Quite simply, by using key passages from the book of Romans, we can outline everything a man or woman needs to know to receive salvation in Jesus Christ. Let's begin.

The Problem

> For all have sinned and fall short of the glory of God.
>
> Romans 3:23

Salvation is *good news*, but it comes to us against a backdrop of bad news. The bad news is this: We are all sinners. Not one man or woman on planet earth—past, present, or future—is without sin.

The Greek word for *sin* literally means "to miss the mark." It describes a bowman who drew back his string, released his arrow, and failed to hit the bull's-eye. Similarly, sin involves missing the target. What is the target? The verse we just looked at tells us: "All have sinned and *fall short of the glory of God*" (emphasis added). Sin is falling short of God's glory—His standard.

To help you understand this concept, I must attack a popular myth maintained by the media, the literary community, and sometimes even the church itself. The fable is that sin can be measured by degree. For many of us, criminals seem like big-time sinners, while those of us who tell little white lies are lightweight sinners. It appears logical to believe that those in the county jail have not sinned as seriously as those in the state penitentiary. But sin looks quite different from God's perspective.

In Scripture, sin is not measured by degree. Either we fall short of God's glory, His standard or mark, or we don't. Since the entire sin question pivots on this point, let's make sure we understand our target.

Any time we do anything that does not attain to God's standard, His glory, any time we fail to reflect the character of God through our actions by missing His standard, we have sinned. There is a story of two men who were exploring an island, when suddenly a volcano erupted. In moments, the two found themselves surrounded by molten lava. Several feet away was a clearing—and a path to safety. To get there, however, they would have to jump across the river of melted rock. The first gentleman was an active senior citizen, but hardly an outstanding physical specimen. He ran as fast as he could, took an admirable leap, but traveled only a few feet. He met a swift death in the super-heated lava.

The other explorer was a much younger, more virile man in excellent physical condition. In fact, the college record he set in the broad jump had remained unbroken to that day. He put all his energy into his run, jumped with flawless form, and shattered his own college record. Unfortunately, he landed far short of the clearing. Though the younger man clearly outperformed his companion, both wound up equally dead. Survival was so far out of reach that ability was a nonissue.

Degrees of "goodness" may be important when hiring an employee or choosing neighbors. But when the issue is sin, the only standard that matters is God's perfect holiness. The question is not how you measure up against the guy down the street, but how you measure up to God. God's standard is perfect righteousness, and it is a standard that even the best-behaved or most morally upright person still cannot reach.

The Penalty

> Therefore, just as sin came into the world through one man, and death through sin, and so death spread to all men because all sinned.
>
> Romans 5:12 ESV

Now, as you read this passage, you may be thinking, *If sin entered the world through one man, Adam, it isn't fair to punish the rest of us.* Yet, death spread to all men because "all have sinned." We are not punished simply because Adam sinned, but because we inherited Adam's propensity to sin and have sinned ourselves.

Have you ever noticed that you don't need to teach your children how to sin? Can you imagine sitting down with your child and saying, "Here's how to lie successfully" or "Let me show you how to be selfish"? Those things come naturally to children.

Let me illustrate this another way. Have you ever seen an apple with a small hole in it? If you do, don't eat it. The presence of the hole suggests that there is a worm in there waiting for you.

Now, most people don't know how the worm managed to take up residence in that apple. They think it was slithering by one day and decided to bore through the outer skin of the fruit and set up house inside. However, that is not what happens. Worms hatch from larvae dropped on the apple blossom. The blossom becomes a bud, and the bud turns into fruit. The apple literally grows up around the larvae. The hole is left when the worm matures and digs its way out.

In the same way, the seed of sin is within each and every one of us at the moment of conception. Though it may take some time before the evidence of sin shows on the surface, it is there and eventually makes its presence known.

Sin demands a penalty. That penalty, according to Scripture, is death. That means physical death (where the soul is separated from the body) and spiritual death (where the soul is separated from God).

The Provision

> But God demonstrates his own love for us in this: While we were still sinners, Christ died for us.
>
> Romans 5:8 NIV

Two very powerful words when put together are *but God*. Those words can revolutionize any situation. "My marriage is falling apart. But God . . ." "My husband abandoned us, and my children are out of control. But God . . ." "I have no job, no income, and no future. But God . . ." God can restore any situation. "I'm a sinner condemned to eternal separation from God. But God . . ." Those same words sum up the Good News for each of us. Even while we were still sinners, God proved His love for us by sending Jesus Christ to die in our place.

How amazing that God would love us so deeply. We certainly have done nothing to deserve it. But the amazement deepens when you consider the significance of Jesus' sacrifice on Calvary.

Not just anybody could die for the penalty of sin. You see, we all have sinned. So none of us could die to pay the penalty of sin because whoever would save us must be perfectly sinless.

Two brothers were playing in the woods one summer day when, almost without warning, a bee flew down and stung the older brother on the eyelid. He put his hands to his face and fell to the ground in pain. As the younger brother looked on in horror, the bee began buzzing around his head. Terrified, he began screaming, "The bee's going to get me!" The older brother, regaining his composure, said, "What are you talking about? That bee can't hurt you; he's already stung me."

The Bible tells us that this is precisely what happened on Calvary. God loves you so much that He stepped out of heaven in the person of Jesus Christ and took the "stinger of death" in your place on Calvary. Jesus hung on the cross, not for His own sin, but for my sin and yours. Because Jesus Christ is without sin, His death paid the penalty for all of us.

How do we know that Jesus' death on the cross really took care of the sin problem? Because of what happened on the following Sunday morning. When Mary Magdalene came to Jesus' tomb, she couldn't find Him there. She saw someone and thought it was a gardener. She asked Him where the Lord's body had been taken. When the Gardener said her name, Mary gasped in amazement. It was Jesus.

In fact, according to 1 Corinthians 15, over five hundred people personally saw the risen Christ before He ascended into heaven.

I am a Christian today because the tomb is empty. If not for the resurrection, our faith would be empty and useless. As the apostle Paul said in the same chapter of 1 Corinthians 15, if Jesus were not raised, we should be the most pitied people on earth. But the fact is, Jesus *is* raised. Now what do we do?

The Pardon

If you confess with your mouth, "Jesus is Lord," and believe in your heart that God raised him from the dead, you will be saved. For it is with your heart that you believe and are justified, and it is with your mouth that you confess and are saved.

Romans 10:9–10 NIV

If good works could save anyone, there would have been no point in Jesus' death. But Jesus knew we couldn't pay sin's price. That's why His sacrifice was vital. For His sacrifice to secure our pardon, we must trust in Him for our salvation.

Believing *in* Jesus means a great deal more than believing *about* Jesus. Knowing the facts about His life and death is mere head knowledge. Believing in Jesus demands that we put that knowledge to work. It means to trust, to have total confidence, to "rest your case" on Him. Without knowing it, you illustrate this concept every time you sit down. The moment you commit your weight to a chair, you have believed in that chair to hold you up. Most of us have so much faith in chairs that, despite our weight, we will readily place ourselves down without a second thought.

If a tinge of doubt creeps in, you might steady yourself by grabbing something with your hand or keeping your legs beneath you, resting only part of your weight on the chair. That's what many people do with salvation. They're reasonably sure that Jesus is who He said He is. However, they hedge their bet by putting some of their trust in their efforts at good behavior, in their church traditions, or in anything else they can do.

You must understand that if you depend on anything beyond Jesus for your salvation, then what you're really saying is that Jesus Christ is not enough.

God is waiting for you to commit the entire weight of your existence to Jesus Christ and what He did on the cross. Your complete eternal destiny must rest upon Him.

You might say, "But my mom was a Christian. And she prayed for me." Praise God. But what about you? Christianity has nothing to do with your heritage. It has nothing to do with the name of the church you attend. It's got to do with whether you have placed absolute confidence in the work of Christ alone.

Where Do I Go from Here?

Have you ever confessed your sin to God and trusted in Jesus Christ alone for your salvation? If not, there's no better time than right now. It all begins with a simple prayer. The exact wording isn't important. What matters is your sincerity. Here's an example:

Dear Lord Jesus, I confess that I am a sinner. I have failed to reflect your glory, and I deserve the punishment that results from sin. Jesus, I believe that you are holy and sinless, that you died on the cross at Calvary and rose from the dead to grant salvation. I now place all my confidence in you as my Savior and receive the free gift of salvation and eternal life that you promise to give to me if I trust you for it. Please forgive me for my sins and grant me eternal life. Thank you for saving me. I want to live my life for you. Amen.

APPENDIX E

THE URBAN ALTERNATIVE

The Urban Alternative (TUA) equips, empowers, and unites Christians to impact *individuals*, *families*, *churches*, and *communities* through a thoroughly kingdom agenda worldview. In teaching truth, we seek to transform lives.

The core cause of the problems we face in our personal lives, homes, churches, and societies is a spiritual one; therefore, the only way to address it is spiritually. We've tried political, social, economic, and even religious agendas.

It's time for a **kingdom agenda**.

The kingdom agenda can be defined as the visible manifestation of the comprehensive rule of God over every area of life.

The central theme throughout the Bible is the glory of God and the advancement of His kingdom. The conjoining thread from Genesis to Revelation—from beginning to end—is focused on one thing: God's glory through advancing God's kingdom.

When you do not recognize that theme, the Bible becomes disconnected stories that are great for inspiration but seem to be unrelated in purpose and direction. Understanding the role of the kingdom in Scripture increases the relevance of this several-thousand-year-old text to your day-to-day living, because the kingdom is not only then—it is now.

The absence of the kingdom's influence in our personal lives, family lives, churches, and communities has led to a deterioration of immense proportions in our world:

- People live segmented, compartmentalized lives because they lack God's kingdom worldview.
- Families disintegrate because they exist for their own satisfaction rather than for the kingdom.
- Churches are limited in the scope of their impact because they fail to comprehend that the goal of the church is not the church itself but the kingdom.
- Communities have nowhere to turn to find real solutions for real people who have real problems, because the church has become divided, ingrown, and unable to transform the cultural and political landscape in any relevant way.

The kingdom agenda offers us a way to see and live life with a solid hope by optimizing the solutions of heaven. When God is no longer the final and authoritative standard under which all else falls, order and hope leave with Him. But the reverse of that is true as well: As long as you have God, you have hope. If God is still in the picture, and as long as His agenda is still on the table, it's not over.

Even if relationships collapse, God will sustain you. Even if finances dwindle, God will keep you. Even if dreams die, God will revive you. As long as God and His rule are still the overarching standard in your life, family, church, and community, there is always hope.

Our world needs the King's agenda. Our churches need the King's agenda. Our families need the King's agenda.

We've put together a three-part plan to direct us to heal the divisions and strive for unity as we move toward the goal of truly being one nation under God. This three-part plan calls us to assemble with others in unity, to address the issues that divide us, and to act together for social impact. Following this plan, we will see individuals, families, churches, and communities transformed as we follow God's kingdom agenda in every area of our lives. You can request this plan by texting the keyword "STRATEGY" to 55659 or by visiting TonyEvans.org/Strategy.

In many major cities, there is a loop that drivers can take when they want to get somewhere on the other side of the city but don't want to go through downtown. This loop will take you close enough to the city so that you can see its towering buildings and skyline, but not close enough to actually experience it.

This is precisely what we, as a culture, have done with God. We have put Him on the loop of our personal, family, church, and community lives. He's close enough to be at hand should we need Him in an emergency, but far enough away that He can't be the center of who we are.

We want God on the loop, not as the King of the Bible who comes downtown into the very heart of our ways. Leaving God on the loop brings about dire consequences, as we have seen in our own lives and with others. But when we make God, and His rule, the centerpiece of all we think, do, and say, we will experience Him in the way He longs for us to experience Him.

He wants us to be kingdom people with kingdom minds set on fulfilling His kingdom purposes. He wants us to pray, as Jesus did, "Not my will, but Thy will be done." Because His is the kingdom, the power, and the glory.

There is only one God, and we are not Him. As King and Creator, God calls the shots. It is only when we align ourselves underneath His comprehensive hand that we will access His full power and authority in all spheres of life: personal, familial, ecclesiastical, and governmental.

As we learn how to govern ourselves under God, we then transform the institutions of family, church, and society using a biblically based kingdom worldview.

Under Him, we touch heaven and change earth.

To achieve our goal, we use a variety of strategies, approaches, and resources for reaching and equipping as many people as possible.

Broadcast Media

Millions of individuals experience *The Alternative with Dr. Tony Evans* through the daily radio broadcast playing on nearly **2,000 radio outlets** in over **130 countries**. The broadcast can also be seen on several television networks, including TBN and Fox Business, and is available online at TonyEvans.org. You can also listen to or view the daily broadcast by downloading the Tony Evans app for free. Over 60,000,000 message downloads/streams occur each year.

Leadership Training

The Tony Evans Training Center (TETC) facilitates a comprehensive discipleship platform, providing an educational program that embodies the ministry philosophy of Dr. Tony Evans as expressed through the kingdom agenda. The training courses focus on leadership development and discipleship in the following five tracks:

- Bible and theology
- Personal growth
- Family and relationships
- Church health and leadership development
- Society and community impact strategies

The TETC program includes courses for both local and online students. Furthermore, TETC programming includes coursework for non-student attendees. Pastors, Christian leaders, and Christian laity, both local and at a distance, can seek out the Kingdom Agenda Certificate for personal, spiritual, and professional development. For more information, visit TonyEvansTraining.org.

Kingdom Agenda Pastors (KAP) provides a *viable network* for *like-minded pastors* who embrace the kingdom agenda philosophy. Pastors have the opportunity to go deeper with Dr. Tony Evans as they are given greater biblical knowledge, practical applications, and resources to impact individuals, families, churches, and communities. KAP welcomes *senior and associate pastors* of all churches. KAP also offers an annual summit held each year in Dallas with intensive seminars, workshops, and resources. For more information, visit KAFellowship.org.

Pastors' Wives Ministry, founded by the late Dr. Lois Evans, provides *counsel*, *encouragement*, and *spiritual resources* for pastors' wives as they serve with their husbands in ministry. A primary focus of the ministry is the KAP Summit that offers senior pastors' wives a safe place to *reflect*, *renew*, and *relax*, along with training in personal development, spiritual growth, and care for their emotional and physical well-being. For more information, visit LoisEvans.org.

Kingdom Community Impact

The outreach programs of the Urban Alternative seek to provide positive impact to individuals, churches, families, and communities through a variety of ministries. We see these efforts as necessary to our calling as a ministry and essential to the communities we serve. With training on how to initiate and maintain programs to adopt schools, provide homeless services, or partner toward unity and justice with local police precincts, which creates a connection between the police and our community, we, as a ministry, live out

God's kingdom agenda according to our Kingdom Strategy for Community Transformation.

The Kingdom Strategy for Community Transformation is a three-part plan that equips churches to have a positive impact on their communities for the kingdom of God. It also provides numerous practical suggestions for how this three-part plan can be implemented in your community, and it serves as a blueprint for unifying churches around the common goal of creating a better world for all of us. For more information, visit TonyEvans.org/Strategy. A course for this strategy is also offered online through the Tony Evans Training Center.

Tony Evans Films ushers in positive life change through compelling video-shorts, animation, and feature-length films and documentaries. We seek to build kingdom disciples through the power of story, using a variety of platforms for viewer consumption. TEF merges video-shorts and film with relevant Bible study materials to bring people to the saving knowledge of Jesus Christ and to strengthen the body of Christ worldwide. Tony Evans Films releases include *Kingdom Men Rising*, *Journey with Jesus*, and *Unbound: The Bible's Journey Through History*.

Resource Development

We foster lifelong learning partnerships with the people we serve by providing a variety of published materials. Dr. Evans has published more than 150 unique titles based on over fifty years of preaching, including booklets, books, and Bible studies. He also holds the honor of writing and publishing the first full-Bible commentary and study Bible by an African American, released in 2019. This Bible sits on permanent display as a historic release in The Museum of the Bible in Washington, DC.

For more information, and to opt in to Dr. Evans's devotional email, text the word "DEVO" to 55659, call (800) 800-3222, or visit us online at TonyEvans.org/Devo.

NOTES

Chapter 1 Created for Kindness

1. Samuel K. Cohn Jr., "4 Epidemiology of the Black Death and Successive Waves of Plague," *Medical History Supplement* 27, (2008): 74–100, https://www.ncbi.nlm.nih.gov/pmc/articles/PMC2630035/.

Chapter 3 The Divine Imperative

1. Tony Evans, *CSB Tony Evans Study Bible* (Nashville, TN: Holman Bible Publishers, 2019), 1074.

Chapter 6 Second-Mile Ministry

1. Quoted in Armand Gilinsky, *Business Strategy for a Normal: Concepts and Cases* (Cham, Switzerland: Palgrave Macmillan, 2023), 5.

2. "Our Values," Culture & Values, n.d., Chick-fil-A.com, https://www.Chick-fil-A.com/careers/culture.

Chapter 9 Rich in God's Work

1. Daniel De Visé, "An 'Average' American Income May No Longer Cut It," *The Hill*, June 21, 2023, https://thehill.com/business/4059025-an-average-american-income-may-no-longer-cut-it/.

2. Jason Lalijee, "Here's How Much the World's Wealthiest, Middle Class, and Poorest Make in a Year," Business Insider, December 7, 2021, https://www.businessinsider.com/how-much-wealthy-middle-class-poor-make-income-per-year-2021-12.

ABOUT THE AUTHOR

Dr. Tony Evans is one of the country's most respected leaders in evangelical circles. He is a pastor, bestselling author, and frequent speaker at Bible conferences and seminars throughout the nation.

Dr. Evans has served as the senior pastor of Oak Cliff Bible Fellowship for over forty years, witnessing it grow from ten people in 1976 to now over ten thousand congregants and over one hundred ministries.

He also serves as president of the Urban Alternative, a national ministry that seeks to restore hope and transform lives through the proclamation and application of the Word of God. His daily radio broadcast, *The Alternative with Dr. Tony Evans*, can be heard on over 2,000 radio outlets throughout the United States and in more than 130 countries.

Dr. Evans holds the honor of writing and publishing the first full-Bible commentary and study Bible by an African American. The study Bible and commentary went on to sell more than 225,000 copies in the first year.

He is the former chaplain for the Dallas Cowboys and the Dallas Mavericks.

Throughout his local church and national ministry, Dr. Evans has set in motion a kingdom-agenda philosophy of ministry that teaches

God's comprehensive rule over every area of life as demonstrated through the individual, the family, the church, and society.

Dr. Evans was married to Lois, his wife and ministry partner of over fifty years, until Lois transitioned to glory in late 2019. They are the proud parents of four, grandparents of thirteen, and great-grandparents of three. Dr. Evans married Mrs. Carla Evans in November, 2023 and they serve the Lord together in Dallas, Texas.